Best Easy Day Hikes
Tampa Bay

Help Us Keep This Guide Up to Date

Every effort has been made by the author and editors to make this guide as accurate and useful as possible. However, many things can change after a guide is published—trails are rerouted, regulations change, facilities come under new management, etc.

We would love to hear from you concerning your experiences with this guide and how you feel it could be improved and kept up to date. While we may not be able to respond to all comments and suggestions, we'll take them to heart and we'll also make certain to share them with the author. Please send your comments and suggestions to the following address:

The Globe Pequot Press
Reader Response/Editorial Department
P.O. Box 480
Guilford, CT 06437

Or you may e-mail us at:

editorial@GlobePequot.com

Thanks for your input, and happy trails!

Best Easy Day Hikes Series

Best Easy Day Hikes
Tampa Bay

Johnny Molloy

FALCON GUIDES

GUILFORD, CONNECTICUT
HELENA, MONTANA

AN IMPRINT OF THE GLOBE PEQUOT PRESS

FALCONGUIDES®

Copyright © 2009 Morris Book Publishing, LLC

TOPO! Explorer software and SuperQuad source maps courtesy of
National Geographic Maps. For information about TOPO! Explorer,
TOPO!, and Nat Geo Maps products, go to www.topo.com or www
.natgeomaps.com.

Project editor: Julie Marsh
Layout artist: Kevin Mak
Maps: OffRoute Inc. © Morris Book Publishing, LLC

Library of Congress Cataloging-in-Publication Data is available on file.

ISBN 978-0-7627-5299-7

Printed in the United States of America
10 9 8 7 6 5 4 3 2 1

For John Hamilton,
a good man and a friend of my father

Overview

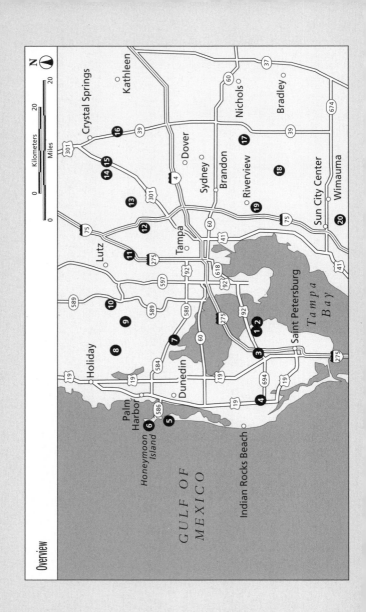

Contents

Acknowledgments

Thanks to all the people who made this book possible. Thanks to Scott Adams for guiding me through this project. Pam Morgan helped all over the place. Nevin Sitler of www.PaddleandPath.com and Billy Reis gave invaluable information. Thanks to John Hamilton for his friendship.

Special thanks go to all the land managers of the area parks and preserves. A special thanks goes to all those who work at Lithia Springs Park. They befriended me and helped shape this book. Finally, thanks to all the hikers in the region, for without you these trails wouldn't have a reason to be, and I would have no reason to explore and enjoy the scenic trails of greater Tampa Bay.

Introduction

Leaning against the live oak, I looked out. Below, the dark stream coursed between palm-lined banks and over limestone rocks, splashing noisily as it followed gravity's orders. Behind me, lush woodland rose to a sun-splashed oak scrub. I considered the biodiversity contained within a stone's throw of my position. It truly was amazing, how—in the space of a few feet—Tampa Bay's ecosystems could vary. I thought of another example on the coast at Honeymoon Island. There, mangrove trees rose from salt water, then sea oats found life above the mangrove. Still higher grew wind-pruned slash pines. I smiled, thinking how the hikes in this book reflect the area's biodiversity.

The greater Tampa Bay area is a watery region. Naturally, people think of aquatic sports when it comes to outdoor pursuits. However, the region is laced with trails that meander along the ample waters and beyond. A quick glance at a map reveals numerous state and county parks, most of which have hiking trails. Beyond that, still other areas have trails on them, particularly the ELAPP (Environmental Lands Acquisition and Protection Program) lands of Hillsborough County. This county has aggressively pursued buying and preserving ecosystems special to the area.

With this book in hand—and willing feet—you can explore the greater Tampa Bay region. The Hillsborough River basin offers many hikes in a junglesque floodplain forest, as well as extensive vistas astride a tributary, Blackwater Creek. The Alafia River basin has hikes that travel along rocky streams and in rare oak and sand scrub environments. Little Manatee River State Park offers a remote watery loop.

1

The urban areas of Pinellas County offer getaways, too—namely Sawgrass Park and Lake Seminole Park, where you can enjoy some lakeside hiking and traversing boardwalks that take you over the water. The coastline is well represented. You must take a ferry to reach Caladesi Island State Park, but it offers hiking directly on the Gulf and the palmy interior of the island. Bird-watchers flock to Honeymoon Island State Park, where you can hike and look for winged creatures simultaneously. Explore the past at Weedon Island. It has the benefit of being a good birding destination, too. Brooker Creek offers freshwater environments and a chance to enjoy some environmental education at its fancy nature center. Other destinations also have facilities for learning about nature, while still other areas, like Violet Cury Preserve, protect lands and have nothing more than a trailhead. No matter where you go, the trails in this book will enhance your outdoor experience and leave you appreciative of the natural splendors of the greater Tampa Bay area. Enjoy.

The Nature of Tampa Bay

Tampa Bay's hiking grounds range from the coastal islands to the high pines and scrub of eastern Hillsborough, from narrow unimproved tracks to paved paths. Hikes in this guide cover the gamut. While by definition a best easy day hike is not strenuous and generally poses little danger to the traveler, knowing a few details about the nature of the Tampa Bay area will enhance your explorations.

Weather
The Tampa Bay area is blessed with a mild climate, with rainy and dry seasons. While overall the weather is inviting, each season poses unique challenges for hikers.

Winter is most conducive to hiking. Including winter's shoulder months, the hiking season generally lasts from November to May, and it can be pleasant hiking weather indeed. Winter days average near 70 degrees, and nights cool down to the 50s. Freezing temperatures are rare, but strong winter winds can make nights chilly. This is the dry season, which usually lasts through May. As the days lengthen and temperatures rise, increasing heat and humidity result in afternoon thunderstorms. These storms become a regular feature in June and last through September. Of course, this is hurricane season also. Gulf breezes occasionally make humid summer days more tolerable. During summer or the shoulder seasons, try to hike early in the morning, when the temperatures are coolest, the sun is lowest in the sky, and thunderstorms haven't had a chance to build.

This area is within the so-called lightning belt, which annually experiences more than ninety days of lightning—when 45,000-amp bolts head from the sky toward the ground. By the time late fall comes, continental fronts are a welcome relief, as they clear the skies and cool the air, and the hiking season resumes again.

Critters

You'll mostly encounter benign creatures on these trails, such as raccoon, deer, armadillo, squirrel, rabbit, wild turkey, and a variety of songbirds and shorebirds from cardinals and sandhill cranes to pelicans and osprey. More rarely seen (during the daylight hours especially) are coyote, wild pig, and opossum.

Tampa's parklands also are habitat for snakes. Encounters are infrequent, but you should be prepared to react properly if you run across a dangerous snake. Snakes generally only strike if they are threatened. You are too big to be dinner, so they typically avoid contact with humans. Keep your distance, and they will keep theirs. In truth, your most negative potential encounters will be with the smallest of critters—mosquitoes and no-see-ums. Wear long clothes and bring insect repellant during warmer times.

Be Prepared

Hiking in the Tampa Bay area is generally safe. Still, hikers should be prepared, whether they are out for a short stroll at Sawgrass Lake Park or venturing into the secluded Black-water Creek Preserve. Some specific advice:

- Know the basics of first aid, including how to treat cuts, bites and stings, and fractures, strains, or sprains. Pack a first-aid kit on each excursion.

- Familiarize yourself with the symptoms of heat exhaustion and heat stroke. Heat exhaustion symptoms include heavy sweating, muscle cramps, headache, dizziness, and fainting. Should you or any of your hiking party exhibit any of these symptoms, cool the victim down immediately by rehydrating and getting him or her to an air-conditioned location. Cold showers also help reduce body temperature. Heat stroke is much more serious: The victim may lose consciousness, and the skin is hot and dry to the touch. In this event, call 911 immediately.

- Regardless of the weather, your body needs a lot of water while hiking. A full 32-ounce bottle is the minimum for these short hikes, but more is always better.

Bring a full water bottle, whether water is available along the trail or not.

- Don't drink from streams, rivers, creeks, or lakes without treating or filtering the water first. Waterways and water bodies may host a variety of contaminants, including giardia, which can cause serious intestinal unrest.

- Prepare for extremes of both heat and cold by dressing in layers.

- Carry a backpack in which you can store extra clothing, ample drinking water and food, and whatever goodies, like this guidebook, cameras, and binoculars, you might want.

- Most area trails have cell phone coverage. Bring your device, but make sure you've turned it off or have it on the vibrate setting while hiking. Nothing like a "wake the dead"–loud ring to startle every creature, including fellow hikers. A GPS with downloaded topographic maps can be an invaluable aid for keeping yourself apprised of your position, especially if used in conjunction with the trail maps provided in this book.

- Keep children under careful watch. The bigger rivers and the Gulf have deep waters and moving currents, and are not safe for swimming. Hazards along some of the trails include poison ivy, uneven footing, hidden cypress knees, and sunny sand flats; make sure children don't stray from the designated route. Children should carry a plastic whistle; if they become lost, they should stay in one place and blow the whistle to summon help.

Zero Impact

We, as trail users, must be vigilant to make sure our passage leaves no lasting mark. Here are some basic guidelines for preserving trails in the region:

- Pack out all your own trash. You might also pack out garbage left by less-considerate hikers.

- Don't approach or feed any wild creatures—the raccoon or crow eyeing your snack food is best able to survive if it remains self-reliant.

- Don't pick wildflowers or gather rocks, antlers, feathers, or other treasures along the trail. Removing these items will take away from the next hiker's experience.

- Avoid damaging trailside soils and plants by remaining on the established route.

- Be courteous by not making loud noises while hiking.

- Many of these trails are multiuse, which means you'll share them with other hikers, trail runners, mountain bikers, and equestrians. Familiarize yourself with the proper trail etiquette, yielding the trail when appropriate.

- Use outhouses at trailheads or along the trail.

Tampa Bay Area Boundaries and Corridors

For the purposes of this guide, best easy day hikes are confined to a one-hour drive from Tampa and St. Petersburg, with all hikes located in either Pinellas County or Hillsborough County.

A number of major highways and interstates converge in the bay area. Directions to trailheads are given from these arteries. They include I-75, I-275, Veterans Parkway, and the Suncoast Parkway.

Land Management

The following government organizations manage the public lands described in this guide and can provide further information on these hikes and other trails in their service areas.

- Florida State Parks, Florida Division of Recreation and Parks, 3900 Commonwealth Boulevard, Tallahassee 32399; (850) 245-2157; www.floridastateparks.org. A complete listing of state parks is available on the Web site, along with park brochures and maps.

- Hillsborough County Parks, 15502 Morris Bridge Road, Thonotosassa 33592; (813) 987-6230; www .hillsboroughcounty.org/parks. They manage not only standard county parks but also ELAPP lands.

- Pinellas County Parks, 631 Chestnut Street, Clearwater 33756; (727) 464-3347; www.pinellascounty.org/park. They manage parks and also Brooker Creek Preserve.

How to Use This Book

This guide is designed to be simple and easy to use. Each hike is described with a map and summary information that delivers the trail's vital statistics, including length, difficulty, fees and permits, park hours, canine compatibility, and trail contacts. Directions to the trailhead, including GPS trailhead coordinates, are also provided, along with a general description of what you'll see along the way. A detailed route finder (Miles and Directions) sets forth mileages between significant landmarks along the trail.

Hike Selection

This guide describes trails that are accessible to all hikers, whether they be visitors or locals lucky enough to live in the Tampa Bay region. The hikes are no longer than 7 miles round-trip, and some are considerably shorter. They range in difficulty from flat excursions perfect for a family outing to more challenging treks in protected wildlands. While these trails are among the best, keep in mind that nearby trails, often in the same park or preserve, may offer options better suited to your needs. I've sought to space hikes throughout the Tampa Bay area, so wherever your starting point, you'll find a great easy day hike nearby.

Difficulty Ratings

These are all easy hikes, but easy is a relative term. Florida hikers can face loose sand, open sun, mucky wetlands, or thick vegetation. To aid in the selection of a hike that suits particular needs and abilities, each is rated easy, moderate, or more challenging. Bear in mind that even the most challenging routes can be made easy by hiking within your limits and taking rests when you need them.

- **Easy** hikes are generally short and flat, taking no longer than an hour to complete.
- **Moderate** hikes involve increased distance and will take one to two hours to complete.
- **More challenging** hikes feature some tough stretches, greater distances, and generally take longer than two hours to complete.

These are completely subjective ratings—consider that what you think is easy is entirely dependent on your level of fitness and the adequacy of your gear (primarily shoes). If you are hiking with a group, you should select a hike with a rating that's appropriate for the least fit and least prepared in your party.

Approximate hiking times are based on the assumption that on flat ground, most walkers average 2 miles per hour. Adjust that rate by the difficulty of the terrain and your level of fitness (subtract time if you're an aerobic animal and add time if you're hiking with kids), and you have a ballpark hiking duration. Be sure to add more time if you plan to picnic or take part in other activities like bird-watching or photography.

Trail Finder

Best Hikes for River Lovers

14 Florida Trail Loop at Hillsborough River State Park

15 Rapids Trail/Baynard Trail Loop

17 Alderman's Ford Preserve Loop

20 Little Manatee River State Park Hiking Trail

Best Hikes for Lake Lovers

3 Sawgrass Lake Park

4 Lake Seminole Loop

9 Lake Rogers Loop

11 Violet Cury Preserve Loop

Best Hikes for Ocean Lovers

1 Boy Scout Loop at Weedon Island

2 Weedon Island Double Boardwalk Loop

5 Island Trail at Caladesi Island State Park

6 Osprey Trail at Honeymoon Island State Park

Best Hikes for Children

2 Weedon Island Double Boardwalk Loop

3 Sawgrass Lake Park

7 Nature Trails at Upper Tampa Bay Park

12 Lettuce Lake Loop

Best Hikes for Dogs

10 Brooker Creek Headwaters Preserve

16 Blackwater Creek Nature Preserve Loop

18 Balm-Boyette Scrub Preserve Loop

19 Alafia Scrub Preserve Loop

Best Hikes for Nature Lovers

Map Legend

═══ ④ ═══	Interstate Highway
═══ ⑲ ═══	U.S. Highway
═══ ㊴ ═══	State Highway
═══ 572 ═══	Local Road
= = = = = = :	Unpaved Road
▬▬▬▬▬▬	Featured Trail
- - - - - - - - -	Trail
∼∼∼∼∼	River/Creek
—··—··—··—	Intermittent Stream
⸺	Marsh/Swamp
⬭	Ocean/Lake
⛵	Boat Launch
⏝	Bridge
▲	Campground
▲	Campsite (back country)
•—•	Gate
🗼	Observation Tower
P	Parking
🅿	Picnic Area
■	Point of Interest/Structure
🚹	Ranger Station
🚻	Restroom
‖‖‖‖‖	Steps/Boardwalk
○	Town
⑪	Trailhead
⚑	Viewpoint/Overlook
❓	Visitor/Information Center

1 Boy Scout Loop at Weedon Island

Natural surface trails lead through a lesser-visited section of Pinellas County's premier bayside preserve, Weedon Island. The hike curves around mangrove-encircled Boy Scout Lake, then traverses upland freshwater forest communities before extending eastward to reach the shores of Old Tampa Bay, where Lookout Point awaits. Your return trip travels the south side of Boy Scout Lake. Be apprised: A power plant north of the trail can lend noise to the experience.

Distance: 2-mile loop with out-and-back extension

Approximate hiking time: 1.5–2 hours

Difficulty: Easy

Trail surface: Natural surfaces

Best season: Nov–Apr

Other trail users: None

Canine compatibility: No dogs allowed

Fees and permits: None required

Schedule: Open year-round sunrise to sunset

Maps: Weedon Island Trails; USGS map: Port Tampa

Trail contacts: Weedon Island Preserve Cultural and Natural History Center, 1800 Weedon Drive Northeast, St. Petersburg 33702; (727) 453-6500; www .weedonislandcenter.org

Finding the trailhead: From exit 32 on I-275, take FL 687 south for 2.4 miles to reach Gandy Boulevard. Turn left on Gandy Boulevard and follow it east for 1.1 miles to reach San Martin Boulevard. Turn right on San Martin Boulevard and follow it for 1 mile, then turn left on Weedon Island Drive to enter the park. Continue for 1 mile to reach the trailhead on your left. There are four parking spots. Trailhead GPS coordinates: N27 51.124' / W82 36.543'

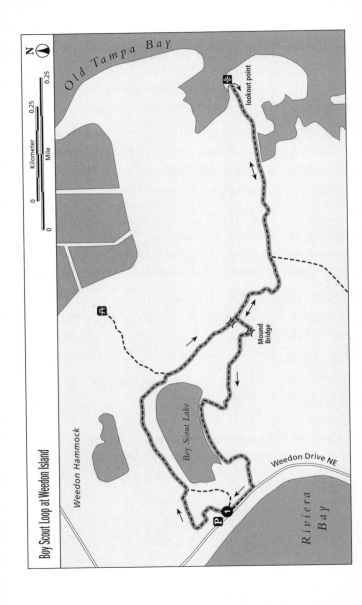

Boy Scout Loop at Weedon Island

Old Tampa Bay

lookout point

Weedon Hammock

Boy Scout Lake

Mound Bridge

Weedon Drive NE

Riviera Bay

P

1

N

Kilometer   0   0.25

Mile   0   0.25

The Hike

This trailhead is reached before you come to the cultural and natural history center at Weedon Island Preserve. The entire Weedon Island experience, including a trip to the cultural and natural history center, is a major Pinellas County outdoors event. The hike follows a dirt, sand, and crushed shell track through numerous environments. At first you will be on a sun-splashed, fire-dependent palmetto plain bordered by scrubby flatwoods. Boy Scout Lake is a major contrast, a salty tidal pond with mangroves crowding its shore. The trail travels a man-made berm, and bridges cross old mosquito control ditches. Beyond the lake the trail's terrain once again reverts to upland freshwater forests. Upon heading toward Lookout Point, you're once again in primarily mangrove woodland while traveling another man-made berm that extends due east through a tunnel of mangroves. The salty tang of seawater drifts into your nose. Freshwater plants grow on the slopes of the berm, even a pine or two. The berm ends at Lookout Point, where you can hear the sea lapping the shore while your eyes gravitate seaward. Your return trip contains a few surprises, including a palm/fern marsh, just one more element of the Weedon Island ecosystem.

Weedon Island Cultural and Natural History Center is the jumping-off point for exploring Weedon Island. Guided hikes and paddling trips on canoe trails, educational programs, and other events can add to your experience. Check ahead and try to combine your hike with an event here. At least take a look around inside before or after your trek. The center is closed on Monday and Tuesday, but the trails are open.

Miles and Directions

0.0   Leave the parking area on Weedon Island Drive and descend just a few feet before reaching a trail junction. Stay left here, circling around the north side of Boy Scout Lake.

0.1   Reach a junction. Boy Scout Lake is dead ahead. Turn left here, traveling under mangroves and palms, with the lake off to your right and a dug canal off to your left.

0.4   Reach a trail junction after turning away from Boy Scout Lake and crossing a short boardwalk. Here, a spur trail leads left 0.1 mile to Picnic Area 2. This hike heads right, away from the picnic area.

0.5   Cross the Five Foot Over Bridge, then reach a trail junction. Your return route heads right, but you stay forward, heading for the boardwalk. Enter upland flatwoods of palmetto scrub with tree islands of pine and oak.

0.7   Reach another junction. Here, a trail leads right toward the natural history and cultural center trails, which include extensive boardwalks. This hike keeps left, heading out toward Tampa Bay.

1.0   Reach Lookout Point. Here, a picnic table provides a good relaxation or lunch spot. Note that the table is attached to a hunk of concrete to keep it from floating away during very high tides or waves. Backtrack.

1.3   Reach a junction. Keep right, going toward the Boy Scout Loop in upland flatwoods.

1.5   Complete the backtracking portion of the hike. The Five Foot Over Bridge is just ahead. Turn left before reaching the bridge; you're now on the Boy Scout Loop, cruising through oaks. Shortly cross the Mound Bridge.

1.6   Pass through a palm/fern flat in a wetland.

1.7   Come alongside Boy Scout Lake. Join a palm-lined berm traveling astride the lake. Shortly leave the lake after making an abrupt left turn. Cross a bridge and continue in upland woods.

1.9 Reach Weedon Island Drive. Turn right and follow the road.

2.0 Reach the trailhead after bridging a tidal stream feeding Boy Scout Lake.

2 Weedon Island Double Boardwalk Loop

This hike travels through Pinellas County's premier bayside preserve. Explore mangrove marsh and island communities, traveling foot trails and extensive boardwalks on historic Weedon Island, where a cultural and natural history center is the focal point for an interactive interpretive education experience that you should combine with your hike.

Distance: 2.3-mile double loop
Approximate hiking time: 1.5–2 hours
Difficulty: Easy
Trail surface: Mostly natural surfaces and boardwalks; some asphalt and concrete
Best season: Nov–Apr
Other trail users: None
Canine compatibility: No dogs allowed

Fees and permits: None required
Schedule: Open year-round sunrise to sunset
Maps: Weedon Island Trails USGS map: Port Tampa
Trail contacts: Weedon Island Preserve Cultural and Natural History Center, 1800 Weedon Drive Northeast, St. Petersburg 33702; (727) 453-6500; www .weedonislandcenter.org

Finding the trailhead: From exit 32 on I-275, take FL 687 south for 2.4 miles to reach Gandy Boulevard. Turn left on Gandy Boulevard and follow it east for 1.1 miles to reach San Martin Boulevard. Turn right on San Martin Boulevard and follow it for 1 mile, then turn left

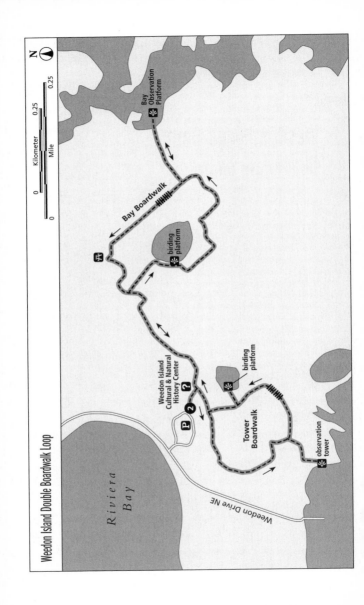

Weedon Island Double Boardwalk Loop

N

Kilometer
0   0.25

Mile
0   0.25

Bay Observation Platform

Bay Boardwalk

birding platform

Weedon Island Cultural & Natural History Center

P
2

birding platform

Tower Boardwalk

observation tower

Weedon Drive NE

Riviera Bay

on Weedon Island Drive to enter the park. Continue for 1.3 miles to reach the cultural and natural history center, on your left. Trailhead GPS coordinates: N27 51.01' / W82 36.36'

The Hike

Weedon Island Preserve covers over 3,000 acres on the west side of Old Tampa Bay. It is the site of 8,000-plus years of human occupation, including an 800-year period where the aboriginals created an oft-studied culture. Today, Weedon Island is enjoyed as a public land. Formerly a state park, it is now managed by Pinellas County. Old Tampa Bay forms the eastern border of the preserve, where mangrove coastal wetlands are a breeding ground for a web of marine life, from the smallest minnow to birds such as roseate spoonbills to mammals such as manatees. The two boardwalks you will travel explore these wetlands. The Tower Boardwalk features a 40-foot-high observation tower where you can look over Weedon Island and note the varied ecosystems. The Bay Boardwalk has an observation platform overlooking a shallow tidal area that is a superior birding locale. Both boardwalks offer extensive interpretive signage about the plants, animals, and human history of the area. The dry land trails travel through pines and scrub forest.

Weedon Island Cultural and Natural History Center is the jumping-off point for exploring Weedon Island. Guided hikes and paddling trips on canoe trails, educational programs, and other events can add to your experience. Check ahead and try to combine your hike with an event here. At least take a look around inside before you begin your trek. The center is closed on Monday and Tuesday, but the trails are open.

Miles and Directions

0.0   From the parking area near the cultural and natural history center, take a short path to reach the asphalt Upland Trail. Turn right on the Upland Trail, away from the center building.

0.1   Reach a four-way junction. Here a trail leads right a short distance to the main parking lot. Keep going straight, now on the Tower Boardwalk. Soon you'll pass the remnants of the old airport building, then join a boardwalk traveling over mangroves.

0.4   A spur boardwalk leads right to an observation tower, where you can gain wide-ranging views of the surrounding coastal wetlands.

0.7   Pass the spur trail leading right to an observation platform over a small pond. Potential birding spot.

0.8   Complete the Tower Boardwalk. Turn right onto the Upland Trail. Pass the cultural and natural history center on the left, heading northeast through palmetto scrub, formerly an airport runway.

1.1   Intersect with the Bay Boardwalk. Turn right here and travel amid mangrove woodland, crossing numerous shallow mosquito-control ditches left over from the mid-1900s.

1.2   A spur boardwalk leads left to a birding platform over a tidal pond.

1.5   Reach a spur boardwalk leading right to the Bay Observation Platform. Here lies a large and shallow tidal inlet, an excellent birding locale. Views are limited to two mangrove islands extending to the east.

2.0   End the Bay Boardwalk to reach a junction and picnic area 2. Turn left here, back on the Upland Trail.

2.1   Reach the other end of the Bay Boardwalk. Head straight toward the cultural and natural history center.

2.3   Leave the Upland Trail. Turn right into the parking area after passing the cultural and natural history center.

3 Sawgrass Lake Park

This hike travels over a mile of boardwalk and more, winding above fascinating freshwater wetlands where huge ferns rise amid widespread maples and substantial sawgrass. Numerous shelters provide resting and relaxation spots. The hike then loops over terra firma in a hardwood oak hammock. The environmental education center at the trailhead is known for its live snake displays, which enthrall children.

Distance: 1.9 miles; two out-and-backs, each with a small additional loop
Approximate hiking time: 1.5–2 hours
Difficulty: Easy
Trail surface: Primarily board-walks, with additional natural surfaces
Best season: Nov–Apr
Other trail users: None

Canine compatibility: No dogs allowed
Fees and permits: None required
Schedule: Open year-round sunrise to sunset
Maps: Sawgrass Lake Park; USGS map: Saint Petersburg
Trail contacts: Sawgrass Lake Park, 7400 Twenty-fifth Street North, St. Petersburg 33702; (727) 217-7256; www.pinellas county.org/park

Finding the trailhead: From exit 28 on I-275, head west on Gandy Boulevard for 1.4 miles to US 19. Head south on US 19 and travel for 0.9 mile to 62nd Avenue North. Turn left onto 62nd Avenue North and follow it east for 0.8 mile to 25th Street North, a residential street. Turn left onto 25th Street North to enter the park at 0.4 mile. Continue to the environmental education center; the trail starts behind the center. Trailhead GPS coordinates: N27 50.325' / W82 40.003'

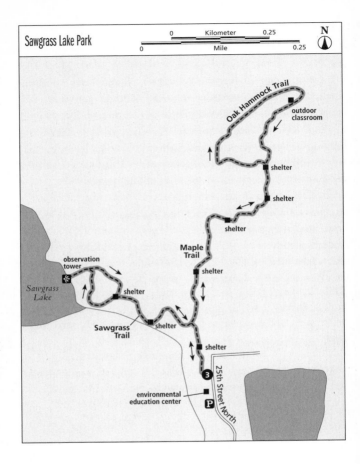

Sawgrass Lake Park

	Kilometer	
0		0.25
	Mile	
0		0.25

N

Oak Hammock Trail

outdoor classroom

shelter

shelter

shelter

Maple Trail

shelter

observation tower

Sawgrass Lake

shelter

Sawgrass Trail

shelter

shelter

shelter

3

25th Street North

environmental education center

P

The Hike

Sawgrass Lake is but one watery element of this park. It is also cut by canals that are popular alligator-viewing areas. But the main attraction may be the wetlands over which the boardwalks travel. All this water adds to the birding possibilities.

You will find other trail travelers relaxing and picnicking in the shelters. If you find one open, stop and enjoy it. In places like these, if you're still, you can wait for the wildlife—especially birds—to come your way. The Sawgrass Trail, the first boardwalk, wanders through sawgrass and among other wetland vegetation in the junglesque swamp forest. You will find the number and size of the ferns to be simply amazing. The trail culminates at the observation tower overlooking Sawgrass Lake. A series of steps rise to a platform with a lake view. After backtracking, you can then enjoy the Maple Trail, which is another boardwalk exploring the park wetlands. The Oak Hammock Trail wanders amid verdant woodland of tall laurel oaks, palms, and ferns. Unfortunately, noise from I-275 can drift this way. Later, the Oak Hammock Trail straddles the margin between swamp and drier forest as it curves around while finishing its loop. The Maple Trail will return you to the trailhead. Try to find new flora on your return route.

Miles and Directions

0.0   From the environmental education center parking area, travel on a sidewalk beneath live oaks to reach a shelter and a canal bridge. Cross the bridge and reach a trail junction. Here, the Sawgrass Trail turns left toward Sawgrass Lake and the Maple Trail turns right. Head left on the Sawgrass Trail.

0.2   Pass a shelter situated on the north side of the canal connecting to Sawgrass Lake.

0.3   The boardwalk splits. Here, head left and pass another shelter, then reach the spur boardwalk leading to the observation tower overlooking Sawgrass Lake.

0.4   Reach the observation tower. Backtrack to the loop, then curve left around its north side. Resume backtracking toward the intersection with the Maple Trail.

0.7 Reach a junction. You are almost back to the environmental education center, but turn left on the Maple Trail. This boardwalk heads northeast toward an oak hammock.

0.8 Pass a trail shelter on your left.

0.9 Pass another shelter. Watch for a huge trailside oak just ahead.

1.0 A spur boardwalk leads right, just after passing a third shelter. It is the continuation of the Maple Trail. Continue straight and join the Oak Hammock Trail. Pass underneath yet another shelter. Here, you will reach the natural-surface footpath portion of the Oak Hammock Trail. Stay left and begin the loop.

1.3 The park's outdoor classroom comes within sight. Keep looping around, nearing I-275. This area can be noisy.

1.4 Pass directly in front of the outdoor classroom, briefly traveling over a brick path.

1.5 Complete the Oak Hammock loop. Begin backtracking and join the Maple Trail.

1.9 Reach the environmental education center, completing the hike.

4 Lake Seminole Loop

This literal walk in the park follows an asphalt path along the shore of big Lake Seminole. Known simply as the Exercise Trail, it offers a natural setting of Florida forest that enables a getaway in urbanized Pinellas County. A shortcut is available to cut the distance in half if you so desire.

Distance: 1.9-mile loop
Approximate hiking time: 1–1.5 hours
Difficulty: Easy
Trail surface: Asphalt
Best season: Nov–Apr
Other trail users: Bicyclists
Canine compatibility: Leashed dogs permitted
Fees and permits: None required

Schedule: Open year-round sunrise to sunset
Maps: Lake Seminole Park; USGS map: Seminole
Trail contacts: Lake Seminole Park, 10015 Park Boulevard, Seminole 33777; (727) 549-6156; www.pinellascounty.org/park

Finding the trailhead: From exit 28 on I-275, head west on Gandy Boulevard (FL 694) for 1.4 miles to US 19. Keep west beyond US 19 as FL 694 becomes Park Boulevard. Continue west on Park Boulevard, which becomes Pinellas County 694, for 5.6 miles to Lake Seminole Park, on your right. Continue winding through the park, and at 0.7 mile pass the boat ramp parking. Jog right here, then continue straight, and at 0.8 mile you will see a sign for picnic shelters 12 and 13, along with a hiker symbol on the sign. Turn left here and park. The asphalt Exercise Trail will be within sight, away from Lake Seminole. Trailhead GPS coordinates: N27 50.719' / W82 46.592'

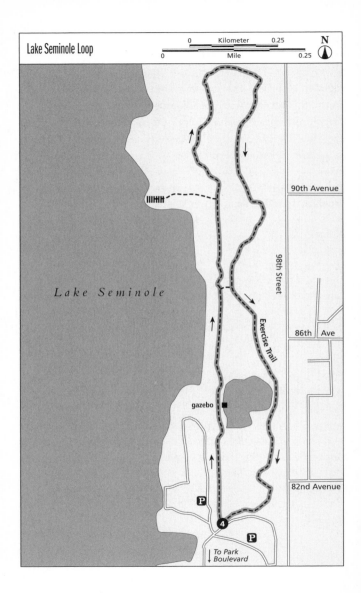

Lake Seminole Loop

Kilometer
0   0.25

Mile
0   0.25

N

90th Avenue

Lake Seminole

98th Street

Exercise Trail

86th Ave

gazebo

82nd Avenue

P

P

4

To Park
Boulevard

The Hike

The Exercise Trail is a popular venue for hikers with a daily regimen, especially those who live nearby in the towns of Seminole and Pinellas Park. Tampa Bay–area residents of all stripes can enjoy this trail, located in well-manicured and eye-pleasing Lake Seminole Park. In addition to the Exercise Trail, it has numerous picnic areas, playgrounds, a ball field, a boat ramp, and also a hand launch ramp for canoes and kayaks. It is truly an oasis of green and worth your time should you pass this way.

The trail's beginning can be confusing. You are likely to see a sign stating End Two Mile Trail Here at what looks to be the trailhead. If you do the entire loop, it is only 1.9 miles, and the sign was put there so people would know when they went 2 miles, which mandates a 0.1-mile overlap. The loop travels clockwise on an asphalt path approximately 8 to 10 feet wide. The trail is also open to bicyclists, and park personnel encourage everyone to go the same direction on the loop, with hikers on the right-hand side of the trail and bicyclists on the left-hand side of the trail.

Gentle curves on the northbound path add to its scenic beauty. Water spigots have been placed in various spots along the trail to keep you hydrated. Tall pines provide partial shade, and palms and moss-draped live oaks provide additional cover. Ferns spread across the forest floor. Hopefully you will have a cooling breeze drifting off Lake Seminole.

Miles and Directions

0.0 With your back to Lake Seminole, walk toward the asphalt path. Once on the trail, walk back toward Park Boulevard and the BEGIN TWO MILE TRAIL HERE sign. Now, begin heading north, away from Park Boulevard, with Lake Seminole off to your left.

0.1 Pass the END TWO MILE TRAIL HERE sign. Exercisers who want to get in the entire 2 miles overlap this 0.1 mile during their walk.

0.2 Pass a smaller unnamed lake on your right. A gazebo offers a shaded resting spot.

0.4 Reach the shortcut leading right to the other side of the loop. Take this trail if you want to travel only 1 mile. Otherwise, continue on the Exercise Trail.

0.6 A boardwalk leads left and extends over wetlands to a viewing platform overlooking Lake Seminole.

0.9 The trail curves away from Lake Seminole, eventually turning back south and passing a park maintenance area.

1.4 Reach the other end of the 1-mile-loop shortcut. Keep south, now under tall pines.

1.5 Cruise past the small lake with the gazebo. A neighborhood is visible off to the left.

1.8 The trail curves back toward Lake Seminole.

1.9 Complete the loop. (**Option:** Continue forward for 0.1 mile farther, going over your tracks, if you want to claim the entire 2 miles.)

5 Island Trail at Caladesi Island State Park

This hike travels through the heart of a Gulf barrier island accessible only by boat. Caladesi Island is the setting for this trek, which travels through coastal strand woodlands before turning into an oak-shaded maritime hammock. The final part of the hike explores the park beach, which in the past has been voted America's best beach. The sandy swath offers shelling opportunities and a chance to hike along a dune community.

Distance: 2.8-mile double loop
Approximate hiking time: 2–2.5 hours
Difficulty: Moderate (slow hiking on sand)
Trail surface: Natural surfaces
Best season: Nov–May
Other trail users: None
Canine compatibility: Leashed dogs permitted; no pets allowed on ferry
Fees and permits: Entrance fee required; ferry fee required unless you have your own boat; no permits needed
Schedule: Open year-round
Maps: Caladesi Island State Park Island Trail Map/Guide; USGS map: Dunedin
Trail contacts: Caladesi Island State Park, 1 Causeway Boulevard, Dunedin 34698; (727) 469-5918; www.floridastate parks.org

Finding the trailhead: From the intersection of Main Street and Alt. US 19 in downtown Dunedin, head north on Alt. US 19 for 2.8 miles, then turn left on Causeway Boulevard. Follow Causeway Boulevard west for 5 miles to enter Honeymoon Island State Park. Continue past the entrance station, then look left for the road leading to the Caladesi Island ferry. Here, a concessionaire offers rides for a fee to Caladesi Island. The ferry leaves on the hour—every half hour

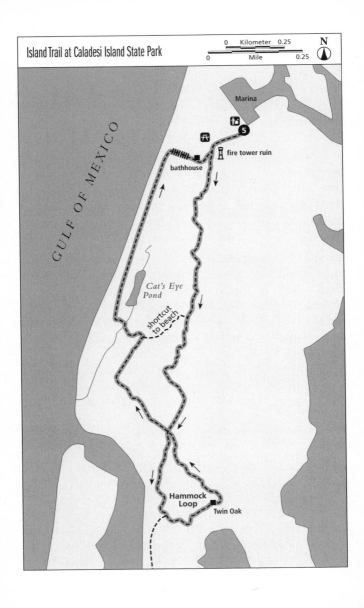

Island Trail at Caladesi Island State Park

GULF OF MEXICO

N

0   Kilometer   0.25
0   Mile   0.25

Marina

5

fire tower ruin

bathhouse

Cat's Eye Pond

shortcut to beach

Hammock Loop

Twin Oak

during busy times—and the ride lasts 20 minutes. For ferry information visit www.dolphinencounter.org or call (727) 734-5263. Once on Caladesi Island, walk around the back of the ranger station and follow the walkway toward the beach. The Island Trail starts near the picnic area, adjacent to the ruin of an old fire tower. Note to paddlers: Caladesi Island can be reached by kayak or canoe from the causeway connecting Honeymoon Island to the mainland. Trailhead GPS coordinates: N28 3.555' / W82 49.220'

The Hike

Here you'll find one of the best hikes in the Tampa Bay area, one of its lesser-used paths. The trail truly does explore much of what the island has to offer, from a historic old fire tower to the history of people who lived on the island to the natural communities here—including coastal strand forest where you walk through nearly pure palm groves. Old-growth pine flatwoods have their place, as does the maritime hammock, where shade is king on this sun-splashed isle. Saltwater environments are represented, too. Walk amid mangroves and over a mangrove-ringed tidal pond. Finally, enjoy the beach. For what is a trip to a barrier island without a stroll on the beach? The beach walk is incorporated into the hike, so you can get in a little bit of shelling or simply kick off your hiking shoes and walk barefoot in the sand.

Interpretive information is placed throughout the trek to help you understand the web of life on a Florida barrier island. The path is well marked and maintained. Much of the trail is open to the sun or only partially shaded, so bring a hat and sunscreen. The sand path can be slow going in places, so factor that in.

Miles and Directions

0.0 Leave the ranger station/marina and walk toward the beach on a concrete path.

0.1 Reach the picnic area and old fire tower site. Look left for the natural-surface trail traveling directly beside the foundations of the old tower.

0.2 Cross a sand service road and enter a coastal strand palm forest.

0.5 Note the unusual trailside palm. It is growing nearly horizontal, then curves upward toward the sky, functioning as a bench.

0.6 Reach a trail junction. Here, a shortcut path heads toward the beach. The Island Trail continues forward, winding through a canopied forest of pines and a few oaks, and it becomes a bit hilly, caused by past mosquito ditching.

1.0 Intersect the Hammock Loop. Continue straight, to the south. Another trail crosses your path—this is your return route.

1.2 A spur trail leads right to a view of Clearwater Beach and now-closed Dunedin Pass. Shortly cross a sand road under a power line and enter an oak hammock.

1.4 Reach an interpretive display detailing the Sharrer family that settled here, and the Twin Oak, a tree split at its base into two trees. Make sure to have your picture taken at the Twin Oak, as island visitors have been doing for over a century.

1.7 Complete the Hammock Loop. You were here before. This time, take the trail leading to the beach, more or less straight ahead, undulating over old dune lines.

2.0 Reach an intersection. Stay left here to immediately bridge Cat's Eye Pond in a mangrove stand.

2.2 The trail opens onto the Gulf of Mexico and the beach. Turn right here and begin heading north along the shoreline. Your exact route will depend upon the tides. This is a good shelling area. Please stay off the dunes.

2.6 Reach the boardwalk crossing the dunes back toward the ranger station/marina.

2.7 Reach the excellent picnic area after passing by a bathhouse.

2.8 Return to the ranger station/marina, completing the hike.

6 Osprey Trail at Honeymoon Island State Park

This hike travels a Gulf Coast barrier island known for its birding and beaches. The Osprey Trail leads through the undeveloped north heart of the isle, passing under mature slash pines before curving along the mangrove shoreline on the Pelican Trail, where you can enjoy watery views. Bring your binoculars.

Distance: 2.3-mile loop
Approximate hiking time: 1.5–2 hours
Difficulty: Moderate
Trail surface: Natural surfaces, including sand
Best season: Nov–May
Other trail users: Bicyclers
Canine compatibility: Leashed dogs permitted

Fees and permits: Entrance fee required; no permits needed
Schedule: Open year-round
Maps: Honeymoon Island State Park; USGS map: Dunedin
Trail contacts: Honeymoon Island State Park, 1 Causeway Boulevard, Dunedin 34698; (727) 469-5918; www.florida stateparks.org

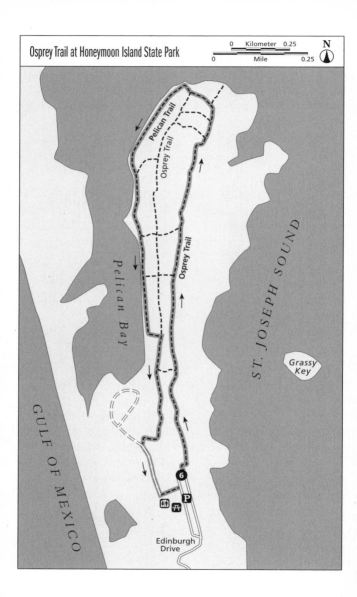

Osprey Trail at Honeymoon Island State Park

0   Kilometer   0.25

0   Mile   0.25

N

Pelican Trail

Osprey Trail

Osprey Trail

Pelican Trail

Pelican Bay

ST. JOSEPH SOUND

Grassy Key

GULF OF MEXICO

6

Edinburgh Drive

Finding the trailhead: From the intersection of Main Street and Alt. US 19 in downtown Dunedin, head north on Alt. US 19 for 2.8 miles, then turn left on Causeway Boulevard. Follow Causeway Boulevard west for 5 miles to enter the park. Continue past the entrance station for 0.7 mile, then turn right at the PICNIC AREA, NATURE TRAIL sign. Travel for 0.3 mile, and you will loop by the Osprey Trail. Parking is just beyond the trailhead. Trailhead GPS coordinates: N28 4.104' / W82 49.818'

The Hike

This hike takes place on auto-accessible Honeymoon Island, a shoreline state park that allows quick escape from the hustle and bustle of Pinellas County. Honeymoon Island was once known as Hog Island before it became separated from Caladesi Island after a hurricane. These barrier islands are always shifting and are subject to not only changes from cataclysmic hurricanes but also the winds and waters that pound daily. This is also reflected in the vegetation. Specifically, the old-growth slash pines are wind pruned at their tops, growing lower in height than their mainland brethren.

Your walk will explore two great environments—an 80-acre old-growth slash pine woodland, and sand and mangrove shoreline including tidal flats and marshland. Interpretive information is strategically placed on the trail to help you learn about birds and other coastal wildlife.

The trail is marked in quarter-mile increments, and contemplation benches are scattered along the path. Numerous spur trails shortcut the loop. The sand and grass path travels amid palms, cedars, sea grapes, and oaks, with a superstory of slash pines. Look for osprey nests in the treetops and among the gray standing tree snags. Not only do these avian aces breed here; the great horned owl also calls it home, and, of late, bald eagles. The eagles have created a major stir among birders, so if the eagles are nesting, a short portion of the loop may be cut off. If this is the case, you can simply work around it on one of the cross trails.

After a mile, the hike joins the sandy Pelican Trail to explore the shoreline. Walk the shoreline where mangroves and sea oats front a great view of the Gulf and beyond. The sandy path makes for slow hiking, but use your extra time to absorb the salty scenery. It's interesting to see the transition from mangroves to sea oats to slash pines as you walk along the shoreline, where this occurs in just the space of a few feet.

Miles and Directions

0.0 Leave the parking area at the north end of the picnic area on the Osprey Trail, soon joining a woods road beneath tall slash pines.

0.3 Reach the first cross trail. Several cross trails shortcut the greater loop. Continue forward on a wide track.

0.5 Reach the second cross trail. Keep north, aiming for the tip of Honeymoon Island.

0.7 Reach the third cross trail. Continue straight under tall pines.

1.0 A spur path leads right to the north tip of the island.

1.1 Reach the Pelican Trail after curving west at the tip of the island. Go right here, joining the Pelican Trail as it heads for the water. The sand path here can be slow going.

1.5 A sand road comes in on the left. Continue forward on the narrowly mown Pelican Trail.

1.6 A spur trail leads left to meet the Osprey Trail. Continue straight, remaining on the Pelican Trail.

1.7 Another cross trail leads to the Osprey Trail. Keep in the margin between the mangroves to your right and freshwater forest to your left. You are now cruising along a small bay to your right.

1.8 Abruptly turn left to leave the water, soon meeting a wide sandy track that is the Osprey Trail. Turn right here, continuing toward the picnic area.

2.0 A service road leads acutely right. Keep south on the heavily traveled path.

2.3 Reach the picnic area. Restrooms, water, and shaded picnic tables are available. Turn left here past the restrooms, following a boardwalk back to the parking area.

7 Nature Trails at Upper Tampa Bay Park

Arguably one of the most scenic recreational areas in the greater Tampa Bay area, Upper Tampa Bay Park is the venue for this nature trail triple-header, where you can enjoy some maritime magic that features multiple environments wrapped up in one destination.

Distance: 1.8 miles along three nature trails
Approximate hiking time: 1.5–2 hours
Difficulty: Easy
Trail surface: Sand, other natural surfaces, and boardwalk
Best season: Nov–May
Other trail users: None
Canine compatibility: Leashed dogs permitted

Fees and permits: Entrance fee required; no permits needed
Schedule: Open year-round 8:00 a.m. to 6:00 p.m.
Maps: Upper Tampa Bay Park Trails; USGS map: Oldsmar
Trail contacts: Upper Tampa Bay Park, 8001 Double Branch Road, Tampa 33635; (813) 855-1765; www.hillsboroughcounty.org/parks

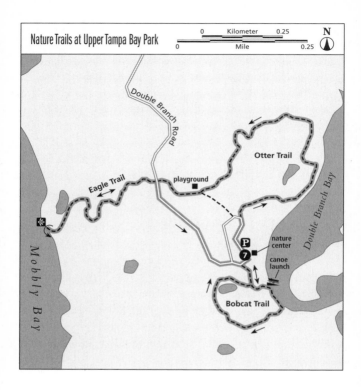

Nature Trails at Upper Tampa Bay Park

0   Kilometer   0.25
0   Mile   0.25

N

Double Branch Road

Otter Trail

playground

Eagle Trail

Double Branch Bay

nature center

P
7

canoe launch

Mobbly Bay

Bobcat Trail

Finding the trailhead: From exit 39 on I-275, take Veterans Expressway (FL 589) to Hillsborough Avenue (FL 580). Head west on Hillsborough Avenue for 6 miles to Double Branch Road. Turn left on Double Branch Road and follow it for 0.4 mile, then turn right to enter the park. Two of the trails start at the nature center, while the other is 0.6 mile along the park road on the right, after entering the park. Trailhead GPS coordinates: N28 0.795' / W82 38.026'

The Hike

As residents know, much of the shoreline along Tampa Bay

has been developed. In fact, this park site was once slated to be a housing project, but Hillsborough County stepped in, so now everyone can enjoy this 596-acre peninsular park bordered by Old Tampa Bay and Double Branch Bay. Three superior nature paths, the Bobcat Trail, the Otter Trail, and the Eagle Trail, explore the preserve and provide an opportunity to see the wide variety of habitats firsthand. Enhance your Upper Tampa Bay Park adventure by bringing your canoe or kayak to paddle Double Branch Bay or bringing a meal to enjoy at the shaded picnic area. Be prepared to hike in the sun, even though plenty of trail passes through shady woodlands.

Start your hiking trifecta at the park nature center. From there, take the Bobcat Trail. This path offers watery views of the estuary against which the nature center is banked. It then circles around a mangrove swamp, along the transitional area where higher ground harbors pines and palms, ultimately returning to the nature center. The Otter Trail, at 0.7 mile, is the park's longest path. It travels through pine flatwoods and open areas of freshwater marsh and saw palmetto scrub, but it also reveals views of the estuary along Double Branch Bay. This trail, like the others, is interspersed with informative interpretive displays, which increase your knowledge of this preserved portion of the bay. This trail also demonstrates how close the transitional environments are—sometimes just a few feet—between mangroves and dry pinelands. The path ultimately turns away from the water and cruises through pinelands before ending. The Eagle Trail is the most remote and least-used path of them all. This out-and-back affair enters an attractive live oak hammock, travels through the palm woods, and finally takes a boardwalk across a freshwater marsh before opening onto Mobbly Bay, which is a shallow bay inside greater Old Tampa Bay. At Mobbly Bay, gain far-reaching views from a platform that has steps leading down to the water. The floor of this shallow inlet will be exposed at low tide, and you may see footprints of people who decided to explore beyond the trail system. Be careful, as the bottom of Mobbly Bay may be mucky.

Miles and Directions

0.0 As you face the nature center, look right for a NATURE TRAIL sign and a concrete path that leads to a loop. Head left, walking clockwise, soon joining a wooden boardwalk, the Bobcat Trail, which opens out onto Double Branch Bay.

0.1 Reach a mangrove estuary. The park canoe launch is visible to the left; keep right along the boardwalk, which soon turns away from the water.

0.4 Complete the Bobcat Trail loop and pass the nature center. Follow the parking-area road to the family picnic area with restrooms, looking for another NATURE TRAIL sign. This is the beginning of the Otter Trail. Walk it counterclockwise. Immediately span a marsh on a boardwalk, and then travel through pine flatwoods.

1.1 The Otter Trail ends at the park playground and the group picnic area. (**Option:** A left turn on a concrete sidewalk at the trail's end brings you back to the nature center parking area.) However, bear right and walk through the group picnic area, then cross the main park road to join the Eagle Trail.

1.2 Enter a live oak hammock where widespread arms of moss-draped trees shade the path. The pungent smell of salt water will drift into your nostrils near Mobbly Bay.

1.5 Meet Mobbly Bay at the Eagle Trail's end. Here, a wooden platform offers a grand vista southwest into Old Tampa Bay. Backtrack to the trailhead.

1.8 Reach the Eagle Trail trailhead. Walk the park road back to the nature center. (**Option:** Backtrack through the playground.)

8 Brooker Creek Preserve Loop

This site combines several well-marked and well-maintained trails at the 8,300-acre Brooker Creek Preserve, in which lie Pinellas County's wildest lands. Leave the fascinating and fancy education center, then head deep into the preserve, traveling a continually changing landscape of forested wetlands, pine flatwoods, cypress swamps, and palmetto plains.

Distance: 4.1-mile loop
Approximate hiking time: 2–3 hours
Difficulty: Moderate
Trail surface: Natural surfaces with a little boardwalk
Best season: Nov–Apr
Other trail users: None
Canine compatibility: No dogs allowed
Fees and permits: None required

Schedule: Open year-round 7:00 a.m. to 30 minutes before sunset
Maps: Brooker Creek Preserve Wildlands Hiking Trails; USGS maps: Elfers, Oldsmar
Trail contacts: Brooker Creek Preserve Environmental Education Center, 3940 Keystone Road, Tarpon Springs 34688; (727) 453-6910; www.pinellas county.org/environment

Finding the trailhead: From the intersection of Tampa Road and East Lake Road in Oldsmar, travel north on East Lake Road for 6.2 miles to intersect Keystone Road. Turn right onto Keystone Road and follow it for 2.2 miles to the preserve entrance, on the right. From the park entrance, follow the one-way road to the education center parking area. The trails start at the covered information kiosk. Trailhead GPS coordinates: N28 8.118' / W82 39.431'

The Hike

Brooker Creek Preserve accurately touts itself as Pinellas County's wildest place. Brooker Creek and its bottomland

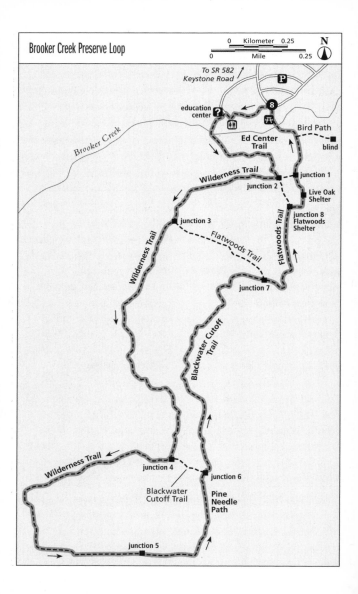

Brooker Creek Preserve Loop

0   Kilometer   0.25

0   Mile   0.25

N

To SR 582
Keystone Road

P

education
center **?**

8

Bird Path

**Ed Center
Trail**

blind

Wilderness Trail

junction 2

junction 1

Live Oak
Shelter

Brooker Creek

junction 3

Flatwoods Trail

junction 8
Flatwoods
Shelter

Flatwoods Trail

junction 7

Wilderness Trail

**Blackwater Cutoff
Trail**

junction 4

Wilderness Trail

junction 6

Blackwater
Cutoff Trail

Pine
Needle
Path

junction 5

hardwood swamps is just one element of the varied hiking experience. This hike will take you through numerous environments that overlap and blend into one another, creating a sublime woodland walk that lends a glimpse into what Pinellas County looked like in days gone by.

This natural area was acquired by Pinellas County in 1992 and has been managed to preserve and restore the natural communities that reside here. It also preserves part of the Brooker Creek watershed, which feeds Lake Tarpon. The environmental education center, opened in 2004, is a top-notch venue with oodles of interpretive information, but it is also the point of origin for getting involved in all the goings-on spearheaded by park personnel.

Mile markers have been placed along parts of the trail to keep you apprised of your distance from the education center. Sand fire roads intersect the trail system but don't cause confusion. The trail junctions are numbered 1 through 8 and help keep hikers oriented. The trail system is kept in the most natural state possible, except for the boardwalks, which protect the wetlands along Brooker Creek. Otherwise, the footing can be uneven, sandy, or rooty. Note that during rainy times parts of the trail system included in this loop will be closed. This is especially true for the southern part of the Wilderness Trail and the Blackwater Cutoff Trail. Call ahead for the latest trail conditions.

Miles and Directions

0.0 From the education center parking area, look for the shaded information kiosk and follow a boardwalk westward through ferns to reach the restrooms, nature store, and education center.

0.1 Reach a boardwalk junction. Here a boardwalk continues forward to the education center, while the white-blazed Ed Center Trail leads left as a boardwalk to span Brooker Creek in a gorgeous forested wetland of wide-trunked hardwoods rising amid fern fields. Shortly leave the boardwalk and travel a natural surface trail through palmetto flatwoods.

0.4 Reach a four-way junction, trail junction 2. Stay right here, joining the orange-blazed Wilderness Trail, traveling west on a sandy track.

0.8 Intersect the green-blazed Flatwoods Trail, trail junction 3. It leads left to shortcut the loop. Continue straight, still traveling south on the Wilderness Trail.

1.0 Pass through a potentially wet area where buttressed pines and cypresses indicate part-time inundation.

1.4 A cypress swamp rises to the left of the trail.

1.5 Reach a three-way intersection, trail junction 4. Here, the Blackwater Cutoff leads left. Stay right on the Wilderness Trail, which now travels west.

1.9 The Wilderness Trail turns south under pines.

2.1 The path curves east.

2.4 Intersect the pink-blazed Pine Needle Path at trail junction 5. Continue forward, heading east before turning north and beginning the return journey to the trailhead.

2.8 Reach a sand road and trail junction 6. Jog right here, take a few steps, and then turn left onto the purple-blazed Blackwater Cutoff Trail. Travel north through alternating dry pines and wetter woodlands.

3.5 Reach trail junction 7. Stay to the right here. You are now on the wide, green-blazed Flatwoods Trail.

3.8 Reach trail junction 8, near the Flatwoods Shelter. Turn right here, joining the white-blazed Ed Center Trail and traveling under mossy live oaks.

3.9 Pass the Live Oak Shelter on your right, then reach trail junction 1. Stay to the right here, still on the Ed Center Trail.

4.0 Pass the Bird Path, which turns right to a freshwater marsh.

and bird-viewing blind. Continue forward, shortly crossing Brooker Creek on a boardwalk. Open onto dry land, passing a picnic pavilion on your left.

4.1 Reach the parking area and complete your loop.

9 Lake Rogers Loop

Lake Rogers County Park, near Citrus Park, is the setting for a loop hike that circles an alluring lake. The natural-surface trail is foot friendly and makes for a great daily exercise venue if you live in this neck of the woods. Even if you don't, the well-kept preserve is worth a trip. Combine it with a picnic and/or a paddle.

Distance: 2.2-mile loop
Approximate hiking time: 1–1.5 hours
Difficulty: Easy
Trail surface: Natural surfaces
Best season: Nov–May
Other trail users: None
Canine compatibility: Leashed dogs permitted
Fees and permits: None required

Schedule: Open year-round 8:00 a.m. to sunset
Maps: Lake Rogers Park; USGS map: Citrus Park
Trail contacts: Hillsborough County Parks, 15502 Morris Bridge Road, Thonotosassa 33592; (813) 987-6230; www .hillsboroughcounty.org/parks

Finding the trailhead: From the Suncoast Parkway (FL 589), take exit 14, Van Dyke Road, and drive 1.6 miles west to Gunn Highway. Turn left on Gunn Highway and follow it south for 1.2 miles to North Mobley Road. Turn right on North Mobley Road and follow it for 0.4 mile to the park entrance and trailhead, on your left. Trailhead GPS coordinates: N28 6.854' / W82 35.340'

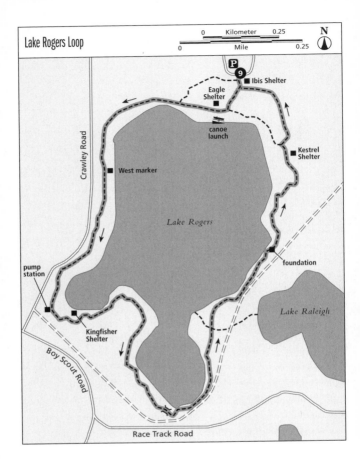

Lake Rogers Loop

0   Kilometer   0.25

0   Mile   0.25

N

Ibis Shelter

Eagle Shelter

canoe launch

Crawley Road

West marker

Kestrel Shelter

Lake Rogers

foundation

pump station

Lake Raleigh

Kingfisher Shelter

Boy Scout Road

Race Track Road

The Hike

This hike makes a wooded and scenic loop around Lake Rogers. The park is enjoyed as a day-use area by locals who like to get their exercise by making a circuit around the lake. The park also has another lake, Lake Raleigh. Several attractive picnic areas are scattered throughout the locale. Also, a canoe launch allows paddlers to explore the shoreline and fish. The 272-acre tract was originally purchased by the city of St. Petersburg as a well field. However, the area is operated as a park by Hillsborough County.

Unlike most lakes in the greater Tampa Bay area, this 92-acre tarn is not ringed by houses, therefore offering a natural respite. No motorized water vehicles are allowed on the lake, which adds to the serenity. Undoubtedly, as urbanization has pushed outward, this area would have been developed, so the thirst of St. Petersburg has turned out to be a plus for hikers.

The trail is wooded for perhaps 80 percent of its distance, providing ample shade on a warm afternoon. It is marked in quarter-mile increments, keeping you apprised of your progress. Interpretive signage is periodically placed along the path, detailing local plants and animals. From the parking lot it isn't long before you reach the lake's edge and pass the canoe launch. By the way, the first trail that circled Lake Rogers was rerouted. The lake's development as a well field affected the water table and lowered the water level, changing the lake in appearance and fact. Eventually the decision was made to pump water back into the lake when it got too low, to restore its natural levels. After this happened, parts of the original trail were inundated, so the path was rerouted— and this is the path you can enjoy today.

The wide natural-surface track travels underneath a lush mix of oaks and pines, as well as through open brushy areas. The lake is never far away. If you can't get a view from the main trail, there is soon to be a spur path leading to the water. Many of these spur paths are used by bank fishermen.

After making one circuit, you might want to take a second lap around.

Miles and Directions

0.0   Leave the parking lot and take the wide marked path heading south through woods. Shortly pass the nature trail and the Ibis Shelter and reach the first junction. Turn right here, heading toward the canoe launch. The other way will be your return route.

0.1   Come to a second junction. Here the Fisherman's Trail leads left while the Lake Rogers Trail leads right. Take a few steps and pass the canoe launch on your left and the Eagle Shelter on your right. Begin circling the lake counterclockwise.

0.5   Pass a marker labeled West. A mown path leads to the water.

0.8   Pass the Kingfisher Shelter on your left. Curve out to peninsula of the lake.

1.3   The trail crosses a little wooden bridge. Begin curving back toward the north into the lake. Pass a marker labeled South.

1.5   Reach a four-way junction. A spur trail leads left to the shore of Lake Rogers. Picnic tables stand near the water. A second spur trail leads right to Lake Raleigh. Continue straight on the Lake Rogers Trail.

1.8   Pass the foundation of a forgotten structure. Benches with good lake views are nearby.

2.0   Pass the Kestrel Shelter. Continue straight on the Lake Rogers Trail. Fisherman's Trail leads off to the left.

2.2   Reach the trailhead shortly after completing the loop portion of the hike.

10 Brooker Creek Headwaters Preserve

This hiking loop travels through a 1,111-acre tract that protects the uppermost part of the Brooker Creek watershed, where ample wetlands combine with upland areas to form numerous habitats that merge and meld in an eye-pleasing trailside medley.

Distance: 2.6-mile loop
Approximate hiking time: 1.5–2 hours
Difficulty: Easy
Trail surface: Natural surfaces
Best season: Nov–Apr
Other trail users: None
Canine compatibility: Leashed dogs permitted
Fees and permits: None required

Schedule: Open year-round sunrise to sunset
Maps: Brooker Creek Headwaters Preserve; USGS map: Odessa
Trail contacts: Hillsborough County Parks, 15502 Morris Bridge Road, Thonotosassa 33592; (813) 987-6230; www .hillsboroughcounty.org/parks

Finding the trailhead: From the Suncoast Parkway (FL 589), take exit 14, Van Dyke Road, and travel 0.2 mile west to Ramblewood Road. Turn right on Ramblewood Road and follow it for 0.5 mile to the nature preserve entrance on your left. Trailhead GPS coordinates: N28 8.211' / W82 33.325'

The Hike

The preserve is approximately 60 percent wetland and thus is an important aquifer recharge area. For the hiker this means you may get your feet wet during the rainy

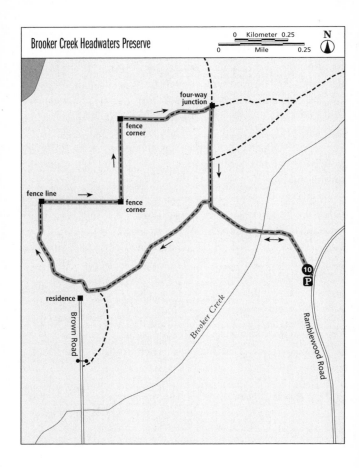

summer season, but I don't recommend hiking here during that time. Being mostly wetlands has its upside—it is a chance to explore many different plant communities, from deep cypress swamps to moist grassy margins where pitcher plants can be found to upland areas such as pine flatwoods and oak hammocks. The area, purchased in the 1990s, is still undergoing habitat restoration. A practiced eye can see the linear row cropping from its days as a pine or orange plantation. The former pasturelands are a little more obvious. Nevertheless, wildlife such as deer, coyote, bobcat, and gopher tortoise find it appealing enough to be home. You will likely find it appealing enough to return after doing this loop and maybe explore other trails here—just don't do it during the wet season or after heavy rains. The easy-to-follow trails mostly follow old double-track roads and are mown wide. Occasional spur trails are generally mown more narrowly.

Leave the trailhead on the old Brown Road, now just an elevated dirt track traveling through rising thick woods, bridging Brooker Creek. The constant variability of the forest is a hallmark of this preserve. It never stays one type of habitat for long, so you won't get stuck looking at the same old scenery over and over like the background from a 1960s cartoon. Before reaching the loop portion of the hike, look below the trees to the left of the trail and find the linear row cropping before it reverted to forest. More row cropping is evident after beginning the loop, while drifting through oak hammocks, sand barrens, and oak scrub, and eventually opening into palmetto prairie with fire-blackened standing tree snags that provide a perfect vantage for the avian set, such as a mouse-hunting hawk. The trail gets a little wetter ahead as it passes through a cypress strand, then travels along the preserve border. Here you can see the contrast—a monoculture pine plantation lies on the other side, and you travel amid natural plant communities, forming a medley of life that extends throughout the trek.

Miles and Directions

0.0   From the parking area, pass through the break in the fence line and keep forward, heading northeast on old Brown Road.

0.2   Bridge Brooker Creek, which can run completely dry. If it is running well, then parts of the trail may be wet.

0.4   Reach the loop portion of the hike at a junction. To the right, your return route heads north. Another trail heads due west. Walk just a few feet down the trail heading west, then split left on yet another trail, heading southwest but still on old Brown Road.

0.8   Pass the spur trail leading left to the trailhead access on Brown Road. Just ahead the trail curves past a residence across the preserve border, then aims north toward a cypress strand.

1.0   Reach a trail junction just after passing through the cypress strand. Here, smaller spur trails lead left and right. Keep forward on the wider main track, northbound, and rise to open country with scattered trees.

1.2   Reach a fence line marking part of the north boundary. Turn right here, heading east, passing the spur trail leading right along the cypress strand.

1.4   Reach another junction at a fence corner. A trail goes straight, but this loop turns left here, north, still along the fence line. Note the pine flatwoods to the east.

1.7   Reach another fence corner. Turn right here, heading east and remaining on the fence line.

2.0   Reach a four-way junction in open former pastureland. Turn right here, southbound, toward the trailhead.

2.1   A grassy track leaves left, skirting the northwest side of Brooker Creek. Keep southbound.

2.2   Complete the loop portion of the hike. Veer left here, crossing Brooker Creek.

2.6   Reach the trailhead.

11 Violet Cury Preserve Loop

Enjoy an "urban wilderness" hike in what was once a country retreat of the Cury family. The 160-acre tract, centered by Lake Flynn, lies in the community of Lutz. A series of foot trails and double-track paths explore a surprisingly lush and appealing forest now encircled by residential development.

Distance: 2.1-mile loop

Approximate hiking time: 1–1.5 hours

Difficulty: Easy

Trail surface: Natural surfaces

Best season: Nov–May

Other trail users: None

Canine compatibility: Leashed dogs permitted

Fees and permits: None required

Schedule: Open year-round sunrise to sunset

Maps: Violet Cury Nature Preserve; USGS map: Sulphur Springs

Trail contacts: Hillsborough County Parks, 15502 Morris Bridge Road, Thonotosassa 33592; (813) 987-6230; www .hillsboroughcounty.org/parks

Finding the trailhead: From I-275 exit 53, Bears Avenue, go east for 0.1 mile to US 41 (Nebraska Avenue). Turn left (north) on Nebraska Avenue and follow it for 0.2 mile, then turn right on Sinclair Hills Road. Travel east for 0.5 mile on Sinclair Hills Road, then turn left on North Fifteenth Street. Continue for 0.5 mile on North Fifteenth Street to reach the trailhead on your right. There is limited shoulder parking here. If this is full, there is also access on Sinclair Hills Road, beyond the left turn to Fifteenth Street. Trailhead GPS coordinates: N28 5.919' / W82 26.564'

The Hike

Tampa residents can make a quick getaway into an eye-appealing environment by visiting Violet Cury Preserve.

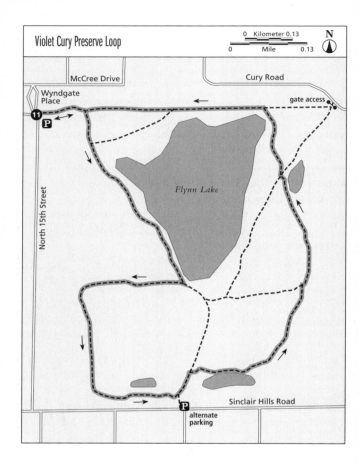

0   Kilometer 0.13

0   Mile   0.13

N

McCree Drive

Cury Road

Wyndgate Place

gate access

11 P

North 15th Street

Flynn Lake

Sinclair Hills Road

P
alternate parking

Those living nearby use it frequently, but most living outside its proximity don't know about it at all. Your hike will harken back to the days when the Curys used this as an escape from the hustle and bustle of Tampa. Can you imagine what they would think now? It's ironic that their former rural retreat still functions as an oasis where people escape the daily rush. Nature's beasts take advantage as well. One regular visitor told me of a fox that calls Violet Cury home.

The well-shaded trail network was developed by a Boy Scout. It combines old roads with narrow single-track paths. Wooden posts and hiker symbols help keep you on the right path. You will also find fire roads used for prescribed burning, which is a difficult thing to do in such a heavily populated area (but to preserve the resource, burning is necessary). Burnings are very infrequent, however, and you will likely find thick woodland of pines and various oaks, and thickets of palmetto, along with a healthy dose of brush and vines, which thrive without burnings. Also watch for impressive old-growth longleaf pines during your hike.

Lake Flynn is a 23-acre natural body of water encircled in marsh grasses. Shoreline anglers use trails to access the lake. A few other smaller, shallow ponds dot the property, and the loop trail travels along these ponds. It's a strange thing when hiking here—your eyes will see wilderness, but the sounds of civilization drifting into the preserve tell you otherwise. Enjoy.

Miles and Directions

0.0 Standing at the intersection of 162 Avenue and North Fifteenth Street, head east through the break in the wire fence and join an eastbound trail as it travels under a tall forest of pine and oak. Houses are off to your left.

0.1 Reach a trail junction. The path continuing straight is your return route. You, however, turn right here, aiming for the west shoreline of Lake Flynn. Shortly pass a narrow foot trail leading left that curves along the shore of the lake.

0.3 Come alongside Lake Flynn, with grassy shore to your left and thick woods, including live oaks, off your right. Continue traveling southeast on a sandy track.

0.5 Reach a trail junction on the southwest side of the lake. To maximize your loop, turn right here, following a woodsy double track due west under younger live oaks shading the path.

0.6 The trail turns south, toward Sinclair Hills Road.

0.8 Just before reaching Sinclair Hills Road, the trail turns left into thick woods as a single-track path. Note the magnolia trees as the trail runs parallel to Sinclair Hills Road. Ahead, pass a small grassy pond to your left.

0.9 Reach a trail junction. To your right a path leads just a short distance to the alternate access on Sinclair Hills Road. Turn left here, heading away from the Sinclair Hills Road access.

1.0 Reach a trail junction. Take the narrow path leading right that soon travels alongside a pond.

1.3 Reach a trail junction. Here, a wide trail leads left back to the south side of Lake Flynn. A firebreak leads right to the preserve property line. Continue forward on a single-track path that dips into an old dredged ditch.

1.5 Reach a four-way junction with a pond off to your right. The most used trail angles right to a gate access off Cury Road. The trail leading acutely left heads to the east side of Lake Flynn. Continue straight on a slender footpath skirting the northeast side of the lake.

1.7 Join a roadbed leading west along the preserve fence line. The lake is to your left and houses are to your right.

1.8 Pass a narrow spur trail leading left along the lake. Continue straight on wider track astride preserve boundary.

2.0 Complete the loop portion of the hike. Continue straight.

2.1 Reach the trailhead.

12 Lettuce Lake Loop

This busy Tampa park is set on the banks of the Hillsborough River and adjacent wetlands. Its hallmark is 3,500 feet of boardwalk that explores interesting riverside wetlands, including Lettuce Lake, a slough of the Hillsborough River. An observation tower avails views of hardwood swamp and water beyond. This area is also known for its birding.

Distance: 2-mile loop
Approximate hiking time: 1–1.5 hours
Difficulty: Easy
Trail surface: Boardwalk, natural surfaces, asphalt
Best season: Nov–May
Other trail users: Parts of hike are also open to bicyclists
Canine compatibility: Leashed dogs permitted on trails but not allowed on boardwalks

Fees and permits: Entry fee required; no permits needed
Schedule: Open year-round 8:00 a.m. to sunset
Maps: Lettuce Lake Park; USGS maps: Thonotosassa, Sulphur Springs
Trail contacts: Hillsborough County Parks, 15502 Morris Bridge Road, Thonotosassa 33592; (813) 987-6230; www .hillsboroughcounty.org/parks

Finding the trailhead: From I-75 exit 266 (Fletcher Avenue, County Road 582A), take Fletcher Avenue west for 1.2 miles to Lettuce Lake Park. Do not turn right on Lettuce Lake Parkway, which is just before the right turn into the park. Inside the park, continue forward to a T intersection; turn left, then take your first right to park. Walk into the visitor center, obtain a trail map, and then begin the hike at the boardwalk in the back of the visitor center. Trailhead GPS coordinates: N28 4.420' / W82 22.463'

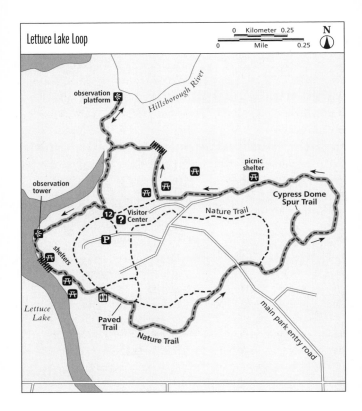

0   Kilometer   0.25

0   Mile   0.25

N

Hillsborough River

observation platform

picnic shelter

observation tower

Cypress Dome Spur Trail

Nature Trail

12   Visitor Center

P

shelters

Lettuce Lake

Paved Trail

Nature Trail

main park entry road

The Hike

Lettuce Lake packs several trails into its small area. It has 3,500 feet of boardwalk, a mile of natural-surface nature trails, and a 1.25-mile paved path open to walkers, hikers, and bicyclers. This hike incorporates all three of the trail types as it explores the park. On your first trip here, make sure to stop at the visitor center, not only to obtain a map but to see the displays and information inside. Get the Lettuce Lake Boardwalk Guide to enhance your learning. More than half of the park is in the floodplain of the Hillsborough River and is thus periodically inundated. The balance of the park is composed of hardwood hammocks and pine flatwoods. Having three plant communities in such close proximity provides maximum biodiversity on this loop.

The hike leaves the visitor center and works its way along the south shore of Lettuce Lake, shortly coming to the observation tower, located at the point where Lettuce Lake meets the Hillsborough River. You can look down on the cypress trees, water ash, and water locust, among other vegetation. By the way, Lettuce Lake got its name from a small floating plant called water lettuce that grows here. You'll also see duck moss and water lilies at times. It's hard to miss the huge cypress trees about. Some are more than a thousand years old! The adjacent cypress knees are amazing themselves. Also look for younger cypresses that are growing directly out of the trunks of decayed and fallen cypresses.

Beyond the boardwalk, you will be going off and on the Paved Trail. This path is a popular training venue and can be quite busy. It—like all the other paths here—is well maintained and groomed. Other parts of the loop join the lesser-used Nature Trail. Finally, near the visitor center, you will join a second boardwalk. This one leads through the swamp and along the upper section of Lettuce Lake, and finally to an overlook of the Hillsborough River. A little bit of backtracking will return you to the visitor center.

Miles and Directions

0.0 Walk out the back of the visitor center and look left for the wooden boardwalk. Reach the boardwalk and head left toward the observation tower.

0.2 Reach the observation tower. A series of steps leads up to the viewing location. Look out on Lettuce Lake and at the wooded swamp below the boardwalk.

0.3 Leave the boardwalk, joining a crushed shell path, passing three picnic shelters before reaching the Paved Trail. Turn right on the Paved Trail and walk past some restrooms.

0.4 Leave the Paved Trail right, joining the natural-surface Nature Trail as it cruises through live oaks and pines with a head-high palmetto understory.

0.7 Rejoin the Paved Trail. Turn right here and soon cross the main park entrance road. Shortly after, the Nature Trail leaves left. Continue straight.

0.9 To the left is the Cypress Dome Spur Trail, a boardwalk that enters the heart of a cypress dome. This is worth checking out. Afterward, backtrack and continue to circle around on the Paved Trail.

1.2 Pass a trio of picnic shelters.

1.4 Turn right on the boardwalk that splits two picnic shelters.

1.6 Intersect another boardwalk. Turn right for an out-and-back trip to an observation platform overlooking the Hillsborough River.

2.0 Return to the visitor center.

13 Nature Trails at Morris Bridge Park

Three trails combine to form a great hike and a way to figuratively immerse yourself in the Hillsborough River ecosystem, located at Morris Bridge in the heart of Wilderness Park. The first travels along the river in cypress woodland. The second loops around a boardwalk, and the third wanders amid swamp woods.

Distance: 2.5 miles on three trails, plus 0.4-mile connector walking

Approximate hiking time: 2–2.5 hours

Difficulty: Easy

Trail surface: Natural surfaces and boardwalks

Best season: Nov–Apr

Other trail users: Mountain bikers on one short stretch of Bald Cypress Trail

Canine compatibility: Leashed dogs permitted

Fees and permits: Donation requested; no permits required

Schedule: Open year-round sunrise to sunset

Maps: Wilderness Park Trails; USGS map: Thonotosassa

Trail contacts: Hillsborough County Parks, 15502 Morris Bridge Road, Thonotosassa 33592; (813) 987-6230; www .hillsboroughcounty.org/parks

Finding the trailhead: From I-75 exit 266, Fletcher Avenue, take Morris Bridge Road east (Fletcher Avenue heads west) for 3.7 miles to Morris Bridge Park. Once at the park, turn right (not left toward the boat launch). Trailhead GPS coordinates: N28 5.839' / W82 18.688'

The Hike

Morris Bridge Park is but one unit of the 7,200–acre Wilderness Park, and Wilderness Park is but one part of 16,000–acre Lower Hillsborough Flood Detention Area. This adds up to the largest swath of public land in the greater Tampa

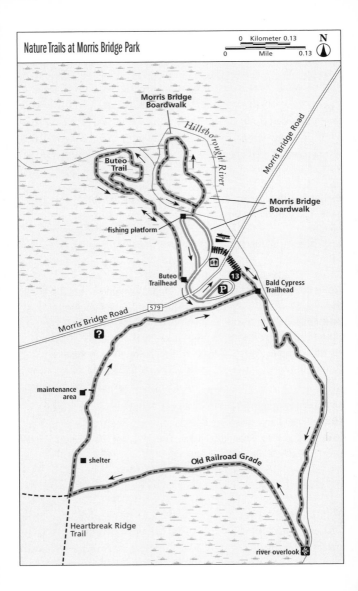

Nature Trails at Morris Bridge Park

0   Kilometer 0.13

0   Mile   0.13

N

Morris Bridge Boardwalk

Hillsborough River

Morris Bridge Road

Buteo Trail

Morris Bridge Boardwalk

fishing platform

Buteo Trailhead

13

Bald Cypress Trailhead

P

Morris Bridge Road   579

?

maintenance area

shelter

Old Railroad Grade

Heartbreak Ridge Trail

river overlook

Bay area. The hiking, mountain biking, and paddling opportunities are many. At Morris Bridge Park hikers can get a close-up view of the Hillsborough River basin. All three trails here are located in a riverine swamp forest that oozes beauty as it oozes water.

First, take the Bald Cypress Trail. Huge cypresses dominate, along with oaks, palms, and maples. Watch your feet while walking among hundreds of knobby cypress knees rising from the forest floor. After enjoying the river, you will take an old railroad grade that travels above the swamp. Imagine yourself as the train conductor traveling through the brooding wetland in the days of yore.

A boardwalk takes you from this trail along the Hillsborough River to the other side of Morris Bridge Road, where you can tackle the Morris Bridge Boardwalk. This elevated trail crosses a channel of the Hillsborough, then circles around an island, revealing wooded riverine splendor. Tall palms form a wooded cathedral. Take a seat on a contemplation bench. This resembles Florida of old.

The third path, the Buteo Trail, is an interpretive track that travels through a hydric hammock, biologist-speak for a forest in a poorly drained area that is underwater part of the year. It is the least used of the three. The Buteo cruises thick, lush woods for one final river experience. All three trails add up to a decent hike and a great learning experience. Also take note that the park has a picnic shelter and boat ramp in case you want to do a little outdoor dining or paddling in conjunction with your hike.

Miles and Directions

0.0 From the parking area, note the shelter toward the Hillsborough River. Head to the right of the shelter and find the sign for the Bald Cypress Trail. Immediately cross a boardwalk heading upstream with the Hillsborough River, split by an island, on your left.

0.5 The trail comes to the old elevated railroad grade. Climb the grade and walk left to reach the river overlook. Here, you can look down on the water and beyond. Begin following the grade away from the river.

1.0 Reach a four-way trail junction. Mountain bike trails head forward, and the Heartbreak Ridge Trail heads left. You stay right on a wide crushed-shell path in palmetto, soon passing a trail shelter on your right.

1.1 A spur trail leads left toward the maintenance area. Keep right.

1.2 Come near Morris Bridge Road and pass an information kiosk, accessed from the road.

1.5 Return to the trailhead. Head left from here, past the aforementioned shelter, downstream along the river on a boardwalk that passes under Morris Bridge Road. Reach the restrooms and a boat ramp on the northwest side of Morris Bridge Road, then join Morris Bridge Boardwalk.

1.6 Begin looping counterclockwise around Morris Bridge Boardwalk.

1.9 Complete Morris Bridge Boardwalk. Walk toward the entrance on the northwest side of Morris Bridge Road to join the Buteo Trail.

2.0 Begin the Buteo Trail.

2.2 Start the loop portion of the Buteo Trail on a narrow footpath leading right (counterclockwise).

2.5 Complete the loop portion of the Buteo Trail.

2.7 End the Buteo Trail. Return to the parking area on the other side of the road via the connector boardwalk under Morris Bridge Road. Don't cross Morris Bridge Road.

2.9 Reach the parking area on the southeast side of Morris Bridge Road.

14 Florida Trail Loop at Hillsborough River State Park

This hike explores a remote section of Hillsborough River State Park. After leaving the busy day-use area, the hike crosses to the north side of the Hillsborough River and then heads downstream through a swamp forest. Watery views extend for a long distance with an everywhere-you-look beauty. Eventually the hike leaves the river, but it stays in the floodplain woodland, where ancient live oaks and huge cypress trees live. A backcountry campsite is situated along the loop.

Distance: 3.7-mile loop
Approximate hiking time: 2–2.5 hours
Difficulty: Moderate
Trail surface: Natural surfaces with boardwalks
Best season: Nov–May
Other trail users: None
Canine compatibility: Leashed dogs permitted

Fees and permits: Entrance fee required; no permits needed
Schedule: Open year-round
Maps: Hillsborough River State Park Hiking Trails; USGS map: Zephyrhills
Trail contacts: Hillsborough River State Park, 15402 US 301 North, Thonotosassa 33592; (813) 987-6771; www.floridastateparks.org

Finding the trailhead: From exit 265 on I-75, take Fowler Avenue (FL 582) east for 1.2 miles to US 301. Turn left, taking US 301 north for 9.5 miles to reach the park on your left. Once in the park, proceed to parking area 3. Trailhead GPS coordinates: N28 8.118' / W82 39.431'

The Hike

Developed in the 1930s, Hillsborough River State Park

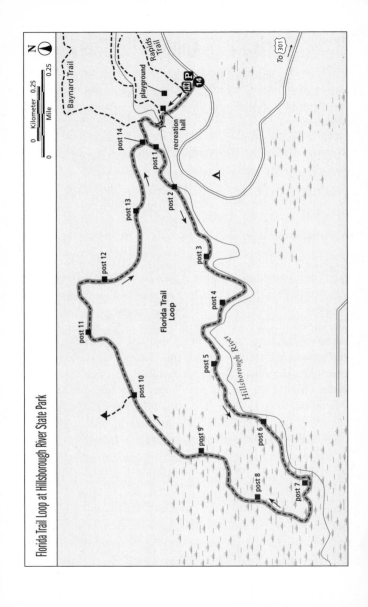

Florida Trail Loop at Hillsborough River State Park

post 14
post 1
post 2
post 3
post 4
post 5
post 6
post 7
post 8
post 9
post 10
post 11
post 12
post 13

Florida Trail Loop

Hillsborough River

Baynard Trail

Rapids Trail

playground

recreation hall

To 301

N

0   0.25   Kilometer
0   0.25   Mile

covers over 3,400 acres of land. The park's amenities enhance an already beautiful setting. It was only later that the Florida Trail loop was laid out, enabling hiking enthusiasts to explore still more of this park, where huge live oaks are cloaked in Spanish moss, their widespread limbs topped with the resurrection ferns, while yet other epiphytes find a place on their limbs.

This hike travels from the most developed area of the park to the least developed. Reassurance markers are posted in ascending order from 1 to 14 along the loop. The hike is shaded most of the route as you pass under a mix of evergreens and hardwoods. The original park management failed to use fire as a tool to keep the park natural, but nowadays they use not only fire but also are working to keep native species reigning throughout the park. This swamp forest is not as dependent on fires as other areas.

Upon beginning the hike, you'll travel on a high berm about 10 to 12 feet above the river. Overflow wetlands drop off away from the water. You can gain view after view of the river that gave its name to the county. Take note of the exposed Suwannee limestone both above and below the water. This rock, along with cypress knees, overhanging vegetation, and clear water, makes this section of the trail one continuous photo opportunity. Turtles will be sunning on rocks and logs, and you may even see an alligator.

Beyond the river, the Florida Trail turns east but remains in the lush swamp forest. This section of trail actually may be wetter than the riverside section, as it travels through low-lying wetlands. Watch your feet—many roots cross the path. Sweetgums and maples are the primary hardwoods here and thus will be devoid of leaves during the winter hiking season.

Miles and Directions

0.0 Leave parking area 3 on a paved path leading toward the primary day-use area. A nearby sign is labeled PEDESTRIANS ONLY. Pass the playground on your right and the recreation hall on your left.

0.1 Reach a junction and the Hillsborough River. Here, the Rapids Trail leaves right. Head left, downstream, to reach the stationary bridge. Turn right on the stationary bridge, and continue on a natural-surface foot trail.

0.2 Reach the beginning of the Florida Trail Loop at a large trailside kiosk with a map of the path you are about to take. The Baynard Trail goes straight. Turn left on the Florida Trail and immediately pass post 1.

0.5 Pass post 2. River views are nearly continuous here.

0.7 Reach post 3 on a bend that allows for good views.

1.0 Reach post 4.

1.2 Reach post 5.

1.4 Reach post 6.

1.7 Reach post 7. The Florida Trail shortly curves north away from the river. Watch for a huge gnarled live oak with just a few live limbs above its thick trunk.

2.0 Reach post 8.

2.2 Reach post 9 just before the trail bridges a slough rimmed with cypress trees.

2.5 Reach post 10 and the spur trail leading left 0.1 mile to a backcountry campsite, located in oak woods.

2.7 Reach post 11 after crossing a streambed via a boardwalk.

3.0 Reach post 12 in less-dense woodland.

3.2 Reach post 13.

3.5 Reach post 14 and complete the loop. Head left and backtrack over the river and through the day-use area.

3.7 Return to the trailhead.

15 Rapids Trail/Baynard Trail Loop

This hike takes place at one of central Florida's most scenic and historic public preserves, Hillsborough River State Park. Walk past a section of rocky class II rapids, then enjoy more all-around forested beauty before crossing the azure river on a Civilian Conservation Corps (CCC)–built suspension bridge. Join the Baynard Trail and loop through a hardwood swamp hammock, finally returning to the trailhead.

Distance: 2.3-mile lollipop loop
Approximate hiking time: 1.5–2 hours
Difficulty: Easy
Trail surface: Natural surfaces with occasional boardwalks
Best season: Nov–May
Other trail users: None
Canine compatibility: Leashed dogs permitted

Fees and permits: Entrance fee required; no permits needed
Schedule: Open year-round
Maps: Hillsborough River State Park Hiking Trails; USGS map: Zephyrhills
Trail contacts: Hillsborough River State Park, 15402 US 301 North, Thonotosassa 33592; (813) 987-6771; www.floridastateparks.org

Finding the trailhead: From exit 265 on I-75, take Fowler Avenue (FL 582) east for 1.2 miles to US 301. Turn left, taking US 301 north for 9.5 miles to reach the park on your left. Once in the park, obtain a park map and proceed to parking area 2. Trailhead GPS coordinates: N28 8.948' / W82 13.754'

The Hike

There's a reason why the Hillsborough River was chosen as one of Florida's first state parks—it is simply one of the most beautiful areas around. Here, the Hillsborough flows

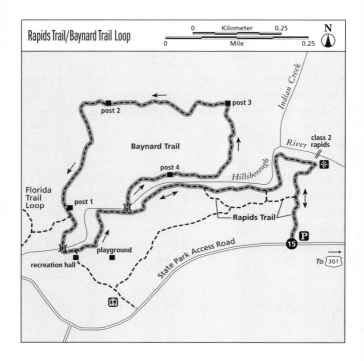

Rapids Trail/Baynard Trail Loop

0 Kilometer 0.25

0 Mile 0.25

N

post 2

post 3

Indian Creek

Baynard Trail

class 2 rapids

River

post 4

Hillsborough

Florida Trail Loop

post 1

Rapids Trail

playground

P

15

recreation hall

State Park Access Road

To 301

through a junglesque hardwood hammock, traveling over exposed limestone, rare in these parts, forming sonorous shoals as it follows gravity's orders in its quest for the Gulf. This was also a strategic spot for a river crossing during the Seminole Wars; the U.S. Army built a fort here in the 1830s. Nearly a century later, the state of Florida established a state park for your enjoyment. The actual parking infrastructure was built by the CCC, and you can still appreciate their work to this day. They constructed some of the trails you will be walking, including the Baynard Trail, which was named after the park's first superintendent.

Note the "Prayer of the Woods" posted at the trailhead. It really reminds you of the value of wood in our society, even to this day. The crushed-shell track is interspersed with interpretive signage to help you better understand the surrounding ecosystem. Enter a resplendent river forest. Soon you'll join the Hillsborough River, traveling along a wooded bluff overlooking the clear water. Boardwalks keep your feet dry in wetter areas. The historic suspension bridge, built in 1936 by the CCC, will take you over the Hillsborough River and onto the Baynard Trail. It also allows a top-down vista of the river scene.

The Baynard Trail travels up the Hillsborough, offering more views from the banks. A series of numbered posts help apprise your position on this lesser-used and slightly more primitive path. The lush palm-pocked floodplain forest continues even after turning away from the river. The stationary bridge takes you back over to the south side of the river and to the busiest day-use area in the park. Here people will be fishing, picnicking, and generally relaxing in a picturesque setting. The best way to get back to the trailhead is to stay along the river, as there are numerous little concrete paths in this area.

Miles and Directions

0.0 Leave parking area 2 on the Rapids Trail. Continue straight, heading toward the Hillsborough River.

0.1 Reach a junction. Here a loop of the Rapids Trail comes in from your left.

0.2 Reach a pair of overlooks on the river. Rocky class II rapids splash below. Stay left, heading downstream along the waterway, passing more overlooks.

0.3 Another part of the multipronged Rapids Trail turns left. Continue going straight along the river.

0.5 Yet another part of the Rapids Trail leads left back toward the trailhead. Continue straight along the river.

0.6 Come to the historic suspension bridge spanning the Hillsborough River. Turn right here and join the Baynard Trail, hiking the loop counterclockwise. Note the USGS water-flow gauge, which measures the flow rate of the Hillsborough.

0.8 Reach post 4. The reassurance posts along the Baynard Trail go in descending order.

1.0 Reach post 3.

1.2 Reach post 2. Shortly, the Baynard Trail curves south toward the river.

1.5 Reach post 1 and the Florida Trail Loop junction. Continue straight here, heading for the stationary bridge over the Hillsborough River.

1.6 Cross the stationary bridge, then turn left, staying upstream along the river as you navigate myriad concrete paths in the busy day-use area.

1.7 Complete the loop portion of the hike when you reach the suspension bridge. Continue straight here, backtracking upriver, passing a few junctions with other parts of the greater Rapids Trail system, along with the class II rapids.

2.3 Reach the trailhead.

16 Blackwater Creek Nature Preserve Loop

This hike stretches over a nearly 2,000-acre swath of land that harkens back to the days of the Florida Cracker cowboy as it travels through a myriad of environments, from cypress domes to palmetto prairies to pine flatwoods to riverine swamp forest. You will be surprised at the far-reaching views to be gained in this ranch-turned-preserve.

Distance: 4.9-mile loop
Approximate hiking time: 2.5–3 hours
Difficulty: More challenging
Trail surface: Natural surfaces
Best season: Nov–May
Other trail users: None
Canine compatibility: Dogs not permitted
Fees and permits: None required

Schedule: Open year-round
Maps: Blackwater Creek Nature Preserve Hiking Guide; USGS map: Zephyrhills
Trail contacts: Hillsborough County Parks, 15502 Morris Bridge Road, Thonotosassa 33592; (813) 987-6230; www .hillsboroughcounty.org/parks

Finding the trailhead: From I-4 exit 21, Alexander Street/FL 39/ Paul Buchman Highway, take FL 39 north for 6.7 miles to Patrinostro Road. Turn left on Patrinostro Road, and follow it 1 mile to reach a dead end. Park under the large live oak. The trail starts at the break in the fence to the south of the road. Trailhead GPS coordinates: N28 7.706' / W82 9.148'

The Hike

Blackwater Creek Nature Preserve is one of Hillsborough County's finer properties, but you would never know it

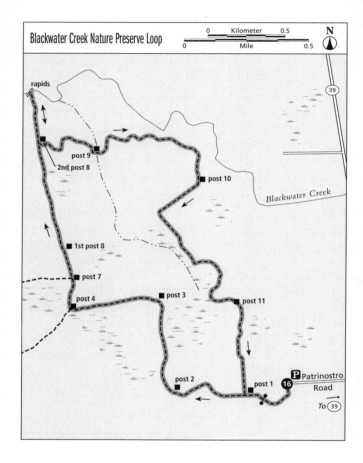

Blackwater Creek Nature Preserve Loop

0   Kilometer   0.5

0   Mile   0.5

N

rapids

39

post 9

2nd post 8

post 10

Blackwater Creek

1st post 8

post 7

post 4

post 3

post 11

post 2

post 1

P Patrinostro Road

16

To 39

judging by the small number of hikers it receives. Perhaps this is because this former ranch still grazes a small number of cattle on the land in exchange for the former owner managing the property. But fear not, for the positive aspects of cruising through this mix of multiple environments is well worth stepping around a few cow patties. This landscape is intensely managed with fire and is also undergoing exotic plant and animal control, all of which keeps this looking like Florida did a century ago. You will walk under majestic live oaks through palmetto prairies extending to the horizon, beneath tall pine flatwoods, and also get a special treat when the trail leads to Blackwater Creek, where a rocky shoal babbles under the shade of a swamp forest. Early-morning visitors may see deer and perhaps sandhill cranes as well as turkeys. The trail itself travels over a series of old ranch roads that are easy to walk. The path is marked with numbered posts for reassurance, hiker symbols, and directional arrows to keep you on the right path. Watch for occasional cattle tracks luring you in the wrong direction. Bring a hat and sunscreen no matter the time of year, as much of the trail is open to the sun.

Once you begin the loop, the multiplicity of environments is immediately evident—oak copses, palmetto thickets, and cypress domes extend in the distance. And the scenery changes constantly. Florida may not have mountains, but it does have prairies, and prairies are where you can gain far-reaching land views, vistas rarely seen in their natural state by modern-day Sunshine State residents. Prairie gives way as you near Blackwater Creek, first evolving into pine flatwoods before the subtle loss of elevation and increased moisture alters the forest to a riverine swamp wood of palm, red maple, and live oak. Take some time and relax, or even bring a picnic to enjoy once you arrive at Blackwater Creek, a tributary of the Hillsborough River. From here, your return trip to the trailhead straddles the margin between the creekside woodland and the open prairie, before crossing more palmetto flats and completing the loop.

Miles and Directions

0.0 Pass through the break in the fence near an information kiosk, then walk south through a field, passing beside a picnic area under two huge live oaks. Climb over a fence stile, then continue curving right around a cypress dome.

0.2 Pass through a gate. A small pond is just ahead on the left.

0.3 Reach post 1 and the loop portion of the hike. Stay left here, rounding the loop clockwise, walking an old double-track roadbed.

0.5 Reach post 2 after crossing in an intermittent streambed shaded by cypress and pines.

1.0 Reach post 3. The trail now curves west.

1.3 Reach post 4 at the edge of an oak grove. Turn right (north), heading for post 7. (**Option:** If you turn left you can add about 1.7 miles to the hike.)

1.5 Reach post 7 in prairie. Continue north, aiming for Blackwater Creek.

1.6 Reach the first post 8, still in open prairie. Continue going north.

2.0 Reach the second post 8. Continue going straight toward Blackwater Creek.

2.3 Make the banks of Blackwater Creek in thick woods overlooking a rocky shoal. Backtrack.

2.6 Reach the second post 8 again. Turn left here, and walk along the nexus of woods and prairie.

2.8 Reach post 9 just before crossing a tributary, likely to be dry in winter.

3.4 Bear right at post 10, meandering southward for the trailhead.

4.2 Reach post 11.

4.6 Reach post 1, completing the loop. Veer left and backtrack past the gate and toward the trailhead.

4.9 Arrive at the trailhead.

17 Alderman's Ford Preserve Loop

This overlooked preserve on the Alafia River, located next to the much more popular Alderman's Ford Park, offers quality day hiking that travels through mixed woodland, open country, and along the Alafia River, with its sonorant rapids. The trail also passes by an old oxbow lake and reaches a historic brick trestle from an abandoned railroad.

Distance: 2.7-mile loop
Approximate hiking time: 1.5–2 hours
Difficulty: Easy
Trail surface: Natural surfaces
Best season: Nov–May
Other trail users: None
Canine compatibility: Leashed dogs permitted
Fees and permits: None required

Schedule: Open year-round sunrise to sunset
Maps: Alderman's Ford Preserve; USGS map: Dover
Trail contacts: Hillsborough County Parks, 15502 Morris Bridge Road, Thonotosassa 33592; (813) 987-6230; www .hillsboroughcounty.org/parks

Finding the trailhead: From I-75 exit 257, Brandon Boulevard, go east for 10 miles to Turkey Creek Road. Turn right and follow Turkey Creek Road south for 3.2 miles to a stop sign just beyond Durant High School. Continue straight at the stop sign for 0.4 mile farther and turn right into the signed parking area. The trail starts at the break in the fence adjacent to the parking area. Trailhead GPS coordinates: N27 52.689' / W82 10.283'

The Hike

Most people in the Tampa Bay area have heard of Alderman's Ford Park. It has a quality 2-mile paved loop trail that locals use for their daily exercise. However, downriver and

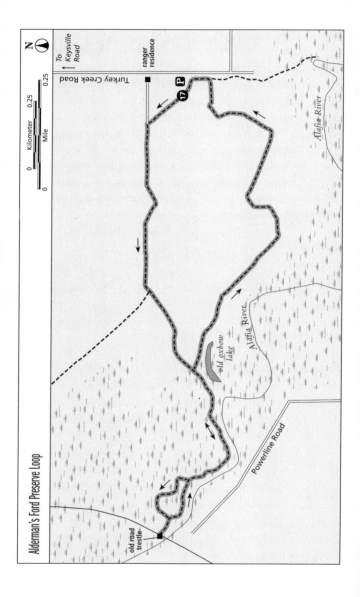

Alderman's Ford Preserve Loop

To Keysville Road

Turkey Creek Road

ranger residence

P

17

old oxbow lake

Alafia River

Alafia River

Powerline Road

old road trestle

N

Kilometer
0   0.25

Mile
0   0.25

accessible from Brandon Boulevard is Alderman's Ford Preserve. This 970-acre tract was purchased by Hillsborough County and borders Alderman's Ford Park on its east end. Along with Alafia River State Park and other property, the public holdings form a 10,000-acre watershed and wildlife preserve that is enjoyed by hikers and paddlers who ply the Alafia. Alderman's Ford Preserve was acquired by the county in the early 1990s but was conveyed to the state of Florida, though the county still manages it.

The hiking trail, marked with posts, arrows, and hiker symbols, travels through former pastureland that is undergoing a restoration to pine flatwoods, sandhills, and wetlands that you can see changing before your very eyes. It is a good viewing area for sandhill cranes, among other species. The habitat restoration is ongoing, and along your hike you'll undoubtedly notice the longleaf pines that are sprouting up in the former pasture area. Make sure to bring a hat and sunscreen since much of the area is open. The stretch of trail along the Alafia River is a real woodsy treat. Here, you will walk along a high bluff, peering into the river below, where fast-moving water spills over limestone ledges.

Travel along the edge of the preserve after leaving the trailhead. Take note of the orange grove just across the preserve fence. Just as sure as the orange grove will become houses, Alderman's Ford Preserve will remain a Hillsborough hiking treasure that will improve as habitat restoration continues. The track passes some massive live oaks before it begins angling downhill toward the Alafia River. Once you're near the river you will skirt an oxbow lake that was once the channel of the Alafia. Don't skip the small loop or the old railroad trestle before backtracking. The abandoned hand-built brick trestle sits silent and overgrown, while nearby modern power lines stretch across the Alafia. On your way back, check out the proliferation of longleaf pines and imagine what this place will look like in thirty years, after careful management.

Miles and Directions

0.0   Walk through the break in the fence. A kiosk is off to your left. A grassy trail heads south, roughly paralleling Turkey Creek Road. You, however, angle right on a different grassy track leading northwest.

0.1   Saddle along a fence line with an orange grove on the far side. Turn left here, heading west. A trail leading back to your right goes to the ranger residence.

0.5   Reach a trail junction. A trail goes right toward the northern part of the preserve. Continue straight toward the river in more deeply wooded land.

0.8   Reach another trail junction. Here, a path leads left. This is your return route. For now keep right, passing an oxbow lake.

0.9   Come alongside the Alafia River, which lies below the bluff upon which you stand. A rapid loudly pours over a limestone protrusion.

1.1   Turn right at the junction. Here the trail makes a small loop, dipping into forested lowland.

1.2   Return to the river bluff. Turn right here and walk just a short distance to the old railroad trestle, located under a modern power line. Backtrack, passing the other end of the small loop.

1.8   Reach the main loop. Turn right here, passing the oxbow lake, cruising the margin between the heavily forested river corridor and the recovering pasture.

2.4   Curve north after nearing a live oak hammock.

2.7   Intersect a trail near Turkey Creek Road. That path turns right (south), and then meets up with the Alafia River. This hike turns left (north) to shortly reach the trailhead.

18 Balm-Boyette Scrub Preserve Loop

This must-do hike loops through one of Tampa Bay's most important preserved parcels. Centered by upper Bell Creek, Balm-Boyette contains not-so-sexy sounding—yet significant—scrub habitat that contains rare species such as the Florida golden astor. Follow a single-track path across Bell Creek, then enter scrub lands, traveling sandy tracks before crossing Bell Creek a second time and returning to the trailhead.

Distance: 3.5-mile loop
Approximate hiking time: 2–2.5 hours
Difficulty: Moderate (due to sandy trail in spots)
Trail surface: Natural surfaces
Best season: Nov–Apr
Other trail users: None
Canine compatibility: Leashed dogs permitted
Fees and permits: None required

Schedule: Open year-round sunrise to sunset
Maps: Balm-Boyette Scrub & Triple Creek Nature Preserves; USGS maps: Lithia, Riverview
Trail contacts: Hillsborough County Parks, 15502 Morris Bridge Road, Thonotosassa 33592; (813) 987-6230; www.hillsboroughcounty.org/parks

Finding the trailhead: From I-75 exit 246, Big Bend Road, go east for 6 miles and turn right on Balm-Riverview Road. Follow Balm-Riverview Road for 2.5 miles and turn left on County Road 672. Follow CR 672 for 1.6 miles to Balm-Boyette Road. Turn left and travel 1.2 miles to reach the trailhead, on your right. Trailhead GPS coordinates: N27 48.309' / W82 14.354'

The Hike

Balm-Boyette may not be the biggest parcel of protected land in the greater Tampa Bay area, but it may be the most

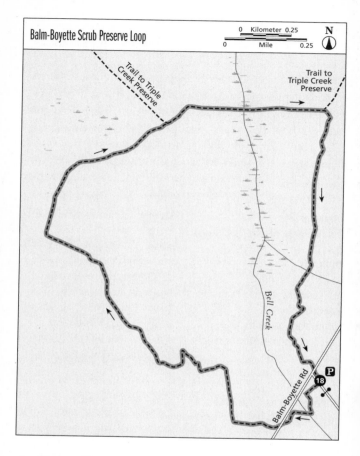

significant. The undisturbed upland scrub habitat, rare to begin with, is even rarer in the ever-expanding greater Tampa Bay area. Covering over 5,700 acres, including the adjacent Triple Creek Preserve, the area protects 800 acres of scrub habitat—broken into several parcels—within its boundaries. It is also known for high numbers of gopher tortoises. Their burrows are important for other critters that inhabit this area, which also includes freshwater wetlands and swamps along Bell Creek.

This hiking trail travels the part of the preserve on the northwest side of Balm-Boyette Road. The southeast-side section is known for its numerous mountain biking trails that travel old phosphate mines. The hiking trail is marked with posts, hiker symbols, and arrows. Along the way, especially in the scrub habitat, it intersects many old sand roads. Fear not; the correct way is well marked. Another trail leaves the upper part of this loop and heads into Triple Creek Preserve. Add a couple of miles to your loop if you are feeling frisky.

Your first surprise will be the lushness of the forest, especially if you're expecting scrub habitat. Instead it heads southwesterly into a deep woodland of bay trees, swamp hardwoods, and ferns of Bell Creek. Soon you will climb away from the stream and enter pine flatwoods before reaching the anticipated scrub. This habitat includes sand pine scrub and the more rare xeric oak scrub. Fire is an important component of the habitat, and the numerous sand roads you cross are effectively divisions used to manage different tracts within the preserve. The scrub lends a real sense of remoteness, rarely found elsewhere in the Tampa Bay area. The forest changes again, regaining its lushness, upon meeting Bell Creek a second time. The final part of the loop is more shaded and cruises over a tributary of Bell Creek before reaching the trailhead.

Miles and Directions

0.0 Standing at the parking area with Balm-Boyette Road behind you, a road gate and gravel road stand in front of you.

Mountain bikers take off for the gravel road. The hiking trail, however, leads right, through a narrow break in the fence beside a kiosk. Immediately join a single-track path in thick woods, and soon you will reach Bell Creek.

0.3 Cross Balm-Boyette Road, step over a fence, and then reach a gate to reenter preserve property. Continue straight on a grassy roadbed.

0.4 The grassy roadbed splits. Stay right, entering pine flat-woods, still on a double-track path.

0.6 The double-track path continues straight while the hiking trail leads left as a single track and winds through a mix of woods and open areas. This area can be confusing, so make sure to follow the posts, hiker symbols, and arrows.

0.8 Open onto scrub and a sand road. Turn sharply left here, heading south, before curving back north. The road separates scrub from oak-dominated woods after turning north.

1.0 Reach a junction of sand roads. Keep right here. You are now in pure scrub environment.

1.3 Reach a junction of sand roads. Keep forward.

1.4 Reach a four-way sand-road junction. Keep forward, aiming for the tall pines in the distance.

1.5 Reach a sand-trail junction. Turn right here, cruising north-northeast along the margin between scrub to your right and high pines to your left.

2.0 Reach a marked trail junction. The path leading left, north-west, heads into Triple Creek Preserve and rejoins this trail later. Head right just a few feet and join a marked shaded path heading left as a sand road continues straight.

2.3 Step over Bell Creek in deep woods. Keep east.

2.5 Reach a three-way sand-trail junction. The path from Triple Creek comes in on the left. Turn right, southbound, amid laurel oak trees.

3.2 Step over a tributary of Bell Creek in thick woods.

3.5 Reach the trailhead after crossing Balm-Boyette Road.

19 Alafia Scrub Preserve Loop

This inauspicious 80-acre tract harbors a primitive loop trail that explores a preserved mosaic of forestland and includes a platform view of the Alafia River and a salt marsh. The preserve is also a haven for native species, as invasive and exotic plants are kept under control.

Distance: 1.7-mile loop
Approximate hiking time: 1–1.5 hours
Difficulty: Easy
Trail surface: Natural surfaces
Best season: Nov–May
Other trail users: None
Canine compatibility: Leashed dogs permitted
Fees and permits: None required

Schedule: Open year-round 8:00 a.m. to sunset
Maps: Alafia Scrub Nature Preserve; USGS map: Riverview
Trail contacts: Hillsborough County Parks, 15502 Morris Bridge Road, Thonotosassa 33592; (813) 987-6230; www .hillsboroughcounty.org/ parks

Finding the trailhead: From I-75 exit 250, Gibsonton Drive, go east for 0.6 mile to Hagadorn Road. The trailhead is at the corner of Gibsonton Drive and Hagadorn Road. There is limited shoulder parking on Hagadorn Road. Trailhead GPS coordinates: N27 51.447' / W82 20.120'

The Hike

People driving along Gibsonton Road may notice Alafia Scrub Nature Preserve—if they notice it—as a patch of woods amid development that keeps growing farther out from Tampa Bay's waters. Back in 1998, ELAPP (Environmental Lands Acquisition and Protection Program) purchased this land in time to add it to the greater Hillsborough

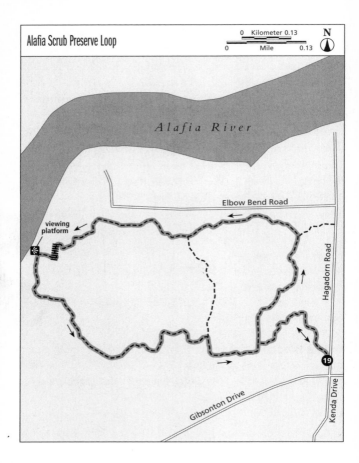

Alafia River

Elbow Bend Road

viewing
platform

Hagadorn Road

19

Gibsonton Drive

Kenda Drive

County park system. The preserve is more important than just a hiking destination; it actually protects a plant community known as oak scrub, which is the most endangered natural community in Florida. The main area of oak scrub is in the southeastern corner of the tract, where the hike begins. It's no surprise that oak scrub would be a rare community in this time, as it is easily developed. But thanks to forward thinking by Hillsborough County, you can walk a very primitive trail through the area, which is surrounded on three sides by homes and businesses, with the fourth side bordering the Alafia River. This section along the river protects a salt marsh astride the waterway.

The trail works around a stile, leaving busy Gibsonton Drive. Though the very narrow single-track path is primitive, it is well marked with posts where needed, with arrows pointing you in the right direction and hiker symbols for reassurance. Vegetation, especially palmetto, can grow thick along the trail, brushing your legs. Consider wearing long pants. The woodland walk is a study in contrasts: The forest gives you a visual impression of remoteness, but the sounds of civilization waft through the trees, belying the illusion of being in the back of beyond. In places, even the visual remoteness is removed with the sight of houses beyond the tract. Even so, in other sections, especially in the wetland palm–live oak hammock near the Alafia River, it looks as if civilization is a thousand miles away. On one hike I saw a snake and a tortoise, so small preserves such as this give not only the plant communities a refuge, but also provide a home to smaller critters.

The Alafia River overlook is a study in contrasts as well. Directly in front of you, the ancient plant called black needle rush, or cord grass, stretches between the viewing platform and Alafia River, which at this point is brackish, rising and lowering with the daily pull of the tides, as it has done for eons. Yet in the distance the traffic of I-75 rumbles over a pair of bridges.

Beyond the river overlook, the trail continues tightly twisting and turning through the preserve, once again entering the primary reason for its preservation—oak scrub—then completes its loop. The final part of the trek backtracks to the trailhead.

Miles and Directions

0.0 Standing at the intersection of Gibsonton Drive and Hagadorn Road, walk through the break in the barbed-wire fence and join the trail heading north as it travels through oak scrub.

0.2 Reach the beginning of the loop part of the hike. Turn right here to walk the loop counterclockwise, leaving the oak scrub.

0.4 Reach a trail junction. Here a short spur trail leads right to Hagadorn Road near some power lines. Pass within sight of Elbow Bend Road.

0.7 Reach a cross trail shortcutting the loop in an open area. The cross trail is also used as a prescribed burn barrier.

0.9 Reach the Alafia River viewing platform after crossing a small boardwalk. The elevated stand extends over a salt marsh.

1.4 Join the south end of the cross trail in an open area. Turn right here on a wide track, then veer left into the woods on a narrow single-track path just before reaching Gibsonton Road.

1.5 Complete the loop portion of the hike. Backtrack toward the trailhead.

1.7 Reach the trailhead.

20 Little Manatee River State Park Hiking Trail

This riverine ramble travels an elongated loop where you can enjoy multiple vistas of the Little Manatee River and the adjoining waterside woodland. The loop then returns through a sand pine scrub forest. Backpackers, take note: A designated campsite is available.

Distance: 6.2-mile loop, with shortcut available
Approximate hiking time: 3–3.5 hours
Difficulty: More challenging (due to mileage)
Trail surface: Natural surfaces with occasional boardwalks
Best season: Nov–May
Other trail users: None
Canine compatibility: Leashed dogs permitted

Fees and permits: Entrance fee; permit required for overnight backpacking
Schedule: Open year-round
Maps: Little Manatee River State Park Hiking Trail; USGS maps: Wimauma, Ruskin
Trail contacts: Little Manatee River State Park, 215 Lightfoot Road, Wimauma 33598; (813) 671-5005; www.floridastate parks.org

Finding the trailhead: From exit 240 on I-75, take FL 674 east for 5 miles to US 301. Turn right on US 301 south for 4.6 miles, then turn right on Lightfoot Road and follow it for 0.4 mile to turn right into the state park. Get your map and a gate lock combination at the park office, then backtrack to US 301. (If the station is unmanned, you need to sign in before your hike and call the park after you have left the hike. Park outside the trailhead gate.) Turn left and follow US 301 north for 1.8 miles, crossing the Little Manatee River. Turn left onto the dirt road located on the east side of US 301, just across from Saffold Road. Open the locked gate and follow the

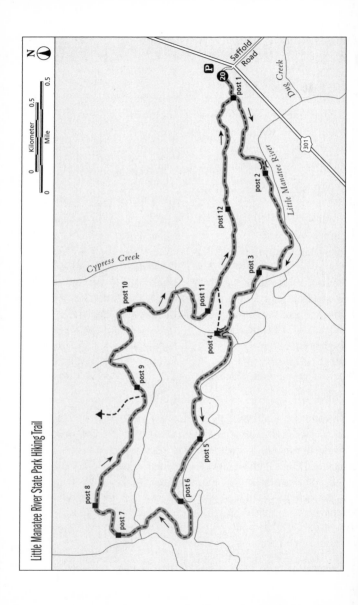

Little Manatee River State Park Hiking Trail

road to a parking area under live oaks. Trailhead GPS coordinates: N27 40.520' / W82 20.964'

The Hike

This is one of the finest loop hikes in central Florida. Built in cooperation with the Florida Trail Association, it is not only beautiful, traveling in deep forests mixed with open areas, but also well marked and well maintained. Numbered posts set out along the narrow single-track trail, ranging from 1 to 12, keep you apprised of your position while traveling the rich riparian margin astride the Little Manatee River.

The beauty begins in a fern field reached immediately after leaving the trailhead. It isn't long before you travel alongside the Little Manatee River, its silent dark waters sliding over a sandy bottom. The riverine part of the trail is tougher than you might imagine, as it often rolls along a berm with overflow swamps on one side and the river on the other. The trail occasionally spans boardwalks and small bridges as it works to stay alongside the Little Manatee. Live oaks, sweet gums, and palms are just part of the riverine vegetation. After a while, state park property lies on the other side of the river, which adds to the wild nature of the hike.

The Little Manatee River is not the only scenic waterway along this hike; the path also crosses Cypress Creek twice. This shallow sandy waterway slides south under rich woods, adding its flow to the Little Manatee. You can actually see the confluence from the trail ahead as it continues along the river. This area also offers your best direct access to the water. At 2.7 miles, the trail finally turns away from the river and passes through a forested wetland of maple and sweetgum, and over an unnamed stream, before rising to sand pine scrub, which differs greatly from the deep woods along the waterway. The trailbed becomes sandy as well.

The hike temporarily loses the wilderness feel as it nears a housing development, but it quickly resumes a backcountry appearance, alternating between sand pine scrub and more lush woodlands. The biggest variation is the hilly area around Cypress Creek. Drift through occasional palmetto scrub mixed with areas of mature sand pines before completing the loop.

Miles and Directions

0.0   Leave the parking area and traverse a fern field along a boardwalk.

0.1   Reach the loop portion of the hike and post 1. Take the trail leading left, and begin the loop clockwise to stay with the ascending numerical posts.

0.6   Reach post 2. Immediately span a wooden footbridge over an intermittent streambed. The trail continues along the Little Manatee River in rich woods.

1.1   Reach post 3. Continue westward on the path.

1.5   Reach post 4 and a trail junction in a live oak hammock. (**Option**: Here, a cross trail leads 0.2 mile to the other side of the loop. The cross trail shortcut will take 3.6 miles off your loop hike.) This hike leaves left, immediately crossing Cypress Creek on a wooden footbridge.

2.2   Reach post 5.

2.5   Reach post 6. Keep along the river as it makes a bend.

2.7   Turn away from the Little Manatee River for good.

3.1   Reach post 7.

3.3   Reach post 8.

3.9   Reach a junction. Here a spur trail leads left 0.2 mile to the designated backcountry campsite, set in an oak dome amid sand pine woods. No water is available.

4.0 Reach post 9.

4.5 Reach post 10.

4.8 Bridge Cypress Creek in a hilly area.

5.0 Reach post 11.

5.1 Reach a trail junction. Here the cross trail leads 0.2 mile to the other side of the loop.

5.5 Reach post 12 amid low-lying palmetto scrub.

6.1 Complete the loop portion of the hike. Turn left to backtrack toward the trailhead.

6.2 Reach the trailhead.

About the Author

Johnny Molloy is an outdoors writer based in Tennessee who spends his winters in Florida. He has averaged over one hundred nights in the wild per year since the early 1980s, backpacking and canoe camping throughout the country, in nearly every state. His efforts have resulted in more than thirty books, covering Florida and a dozen other states, including hiking, camping, and paddling guides, as well as true outdoors adventure story books. He continues to write and travel extensively to all four corners of the United States, participating in a variety of outdoor pursuits. For the latest on Molloy, visit www.johnnymolloy.com.

WHAT'S SO SPECIAL ABOUT UNSPOILED, NATURAL PLACES?

Beauty   Solitude   Wildness   Freedom   Quiet   Adventure
    Serenity   Inspiration   Wonder   Excitement
        Relaxation   Challenge

There's a lot to love about our treasured public lands, and the reasons are different for each of us. Whatever your reasons are, the national **Leave No Trace** education program will help you discover special outdoor places, enjoy them, and preserve them—today and for those who follow. By practicing and passing along these simple principles, you can help protect the special places you love from being loved to death.

THE PRINCIPLES OF **LEAVE NO TRACE**

- Plan ahead and prepare
- Travel and camp on durable surfaces
- Dispose of waste properly
- Leave what you find
- Minimize campfire impacts
- Respect wildlife
- Be considerate of other visitors

Leave No Trace is a national nonprofit organization dedicated to teaching responsible outdoor recreation skills and ethics to everyone who enjoys spending time outdoors.

To learn more or to become a member, please visit us at www.LNT.org or call (800) 332–4100.

Leave No Trace, P.O. Box 997, Boulder, CO 80306